BARRACUDA

FROM THE COCKPIT, No 16

ROBERT McCANDLESS

PUBLICATIONS

Contents

FOREWORD *Rear-Admiral I. G. W. Robertson* CB DSC 3

INTRODUCTION *Lieutenant-Commander Robert McCandless* DSC 4

DESIGN AND DEVELOPMENT *Lieutenant-Commander Robert McCandless* DSC 8
  A Very Clever Design *Commander N. H. Bovey* OBE DSC VRD RNR 14
  Missing Its Generation *Commander David Hobbs* MBE 20

FROM THE COCKPIT *Lieutenant-Commander Robert McCandless* DSC 24
  Nothing If Not Unprepossessing *Captain Eric Brown* CBE DSC AFC 36
  Notes to Ferry Pilots *Courtesy Commander David Hobbs* MBE 40
  Nobody to Say You Nae *Third Officer Joy Lofthouse* ATA 46

LEARNING TO FIGHT *Lieutenant-Commander Robert McCandless* DSC 48

FRONT-LINE FLYING *Lieutenant-Commander Robert McCandless* DSC 58
  Rugged, Complex and Capable *Commander Bertie Vigrass* OBE VRD RNR 64
  No Guns in Anger *Petty Officer Arthur Wells* MiD 66
  Waiting for Vengeance *Lieutenant (A) John Dickson* RD RNVR 68

INTO ACTION *Lieutenant-Commander Robert McCandless* DSC 72
  From Tungsten to Minneriya *Lieutenant (A) Arthur Towlson* DSC RNVR 82

TO BECCLES AND BEYOND *Lieutenant-Commander Robert McCandless* DSC 84
  Hunting Bibers *Commander Andy Phillip* 100
  Katukurunda Etcetera *Petty Officer Roland Spiller* 103
  Change of Plan *Lieutenant (A) John Dickson* RD RNVR 106
  A Little Observation *Lieutenant Keith Davies* 111
  The Last Hurrah *Lieutenant-Commander David Pennick* 112
  Ben Twitch Tragedy *Commander John Neilson* OBE DSC 114

BARRACUDA SQUADRONS 116
  Flown by the Author 140

Above: A factory-fresh Barracuda Mk II photographed up from Brough and on a manufacturer's proving flight; it has yet to receive its radar arrays. The torpedo crutches are prominent beneath the fuselage, but as things transpired Barracudas took torpedoes into action on very few occasions.

Foreword

Rear-Admiral I. G. W. Robertson CB DSC

I JOINED 827 (Barracuda) Squadron on 4 July 1943 as a Sub-Lieutenant (A) RNVR on the same day as the new CO, Lieutenant-Commander Roy Baker-Falkner. I must confess that I went about my business as a pilot in fear and trepidation as the Barracuda was going through a bad time (which the author has faithfully documented). Under the CO's careful and meticulous guidance, we learned to fly the aeroplane correctly—no slip or skid. This I tried to do for the rest of my time on type, and eventually, after squadron service, and as an instructor at the Operational Training Unit as RNAS Crail—a period encompassing two years—I accumulated 373 flying hours and 67 deck landings. These modest figures indicate the trust I had in this aircraft, and why I look back on the Barracuda with affection, as do many others (now a dwindling bunch) who flew this extraordinary-looking aeroplane operationally.

'Jock' McCandless has researched and recorded, through the subject of his book, the triumphs and vicissitudes of the strike element of an arm of the Naval Service that was, at that time, still under suspicion by Their Lordships.

This book is a major contribution to our naval aviation history.

Ian Robertson

INTRODUCTION

Lieutenant-Commander Robert McCandless DSC

I JOINED the Navy in November 1942. The 'Y' Scheme entry was a fast-track route into the Fleet Air Arm with the bare minimum of introduction to seamanship and Naval traditions. At this time, the route was fairly well standardised and literally hundreds of us followed it.

I joined the 45th Pilot's Course at RN Air Station Lee-on-Solent as a Naval Airman II. Many of us on the course were surprised to find that the Navy's shore bases and training establishments had 'HMS' names, and this one was HMS *Dædalus*. The course, numbering about 180, stayed at Lee for four weeks. We were fully kitted out with our bell-bottom, blue-collar uniforms and were then shown how to put them on by a more experienced junior rating. To indicate that we were CW (Commissions and Warrants) candidates, we wore a white band on our round caps instead of the usual 'HMS' which was standard in wartime (the peacetime equivalent showing the name of the ship in which the rating is serving). In Portsmouth, these did not make us particularly popular with the seafaring matelots.

Our accommodation was in prefabricated huts, in each of which about forty of us slept in two-tier bunks symmetrically arranged along both sides and with lockers between. Each hut was heated by a stove in the centre, which, in order to be effective, had to be virtually red hot. The communal ablutions and toilets were more or less as we anticipated—somewhat primitive, to put it mildly.

Regular parade-ground drill was the order of the day with lots of little 'extras' thrown in. Sentry duty with a rifle, no bayonet and no bullets, on the remote access gates around the airfield was not all that popular. However, we were all volunteers and eager to get to the flying part of the sequence as soon as possible, and so did our best to avoid any unnecessary delays by failing to complete everything we were set to do and to the satisfaction of the instructors.

On completion of the programme at Lee, the course moved on to HMS *St Vincent*, the training establishment at Gosport. We were divided into classes of about thirty, and when we were moving around the establishment to different rooms and areas we were required to proceed at the double, carrying our canvas bags containing all our books in our left hands, with elbows straight and firmly by our sides. Different class leaders were detailed in turn, and their job was to muster the class at the morning parade before 'Colours' and report any absentees to the Parade Officer of the Day. During the parade, we all took note of the signal flags at the mast; after the parade they ordered the class to move at the double between the various parts of the establishment as required by the programme. We learned the flags used for signalling between ships, some of which were used in Naval Air Stations and in carriers for passing information to aircraft which had no radio communications and, just to keep us alert, we learned semaphore and Morse.

As far as armaments were concerned, we were introduced to the Sten gun and another similar sized weapon with a wooden stock; perhaps it was the Lanchester. The Bren gun was described very thoroughly and we had to be able to dismantle and assemble the weapon in reasonably quick time, naming all the parts and describing what they did and where they fitted. The 'rear sear spring retainer keeper' has, for some reason, remained in my mind all these years!

One exercise which did not appeal to me very much was pulling a naval cutter up and down Gosport Creek, but it was just another of those Naval things which we were required to experience. There were, however, very many leisure activities too.

In accordance with normal Naval practice, we were divided into two watches, port and starboard, and each watch was subdivided into two parts, first and second. When we were the 'duty' part of the watch we were not allowed to leave the establishment, but when we were not on duty we were allowed to proceed 'ashore'—that is, 'leave the ship'— and we had to do so at fixed times which were referred to as 'liberty boats'. This meant reporting to the 'gangway' five minutes before time, whereupon we fell in and were inspected by the Officer of the Watch; if he was not satisfied, we were sent back to rectify the matter; and if we turned up a minute or so late, we were not allowed to join that liberty boat and had to wait for the next. These rules were rigidly enforced, so they did help to establish the need for

Above: The author as a sub-lieutenant in 1944 (left) with his regular 827 Squadron aircrew companions Leading Airman Ron Hibbs (TAG, centre) and Sub-Lieutenant Bob Smith (observer). Notice the flying rig—no overalls, and a collar and tie!

punctuality: Naval time is five minutes before anyone else's time!

As Duty Part of the Watch remaining on board, we were required to carry out various cleaning jobs and other tasks, one of which nearly put me right off the Navy. I was detailed to report to the Warrant Officers' mess kitchen and the task I was given was to skin a number of rabbits for their next meal. Never having thought about it or seen the job done, I didn't even know how to start. When one of the cooks showed me what to do, I was horrified and when it came to cleaning the animal out I was nearly sick on the spot. I certainly had not imagined that particular experience to be part of flying training.

Introduction to nautical practices and naval traditions was important, but our aim was to become pilots and to this end we received instruction in a variety of subjects such as navigation, meteorology, aircraft recognition and ship recognition.

The eight weeks we spent at HMS *St Vincent* passed very quickly and Christmas was barely noticed. At the end of the course we had to pass exams and as we were all keen to get on to the next stage—flying—there was quite a lot of out-of-hours work put into our efforts to be as confident as we could be on all the important subjects. Anyone who failed the exams was 'dipped' and transferred from the 45th to a later course to go through it all again.

Passing the course was a cause for celebration because it meant that we were actually going to learn to fly, and, to prove it, we wore a 'killick' (an anchor) on our left sleeves. At this time we were issued with our flying kit and thus the exciting proof that we were on our way. Trying on our helmets and fitting the goggles (with a spare pair of tinted lenses and special cleaning cloth to avoid condensation on the insides), the flying suit, the gloves (including a silk pair!) and the lovely soft furry flying boots (which used to slip up and down as we walked and wore holes in our socks)—it was all so *glamorous!* The kit even had its own kitbag, so now on our travels we had two to look after, the huge brown one with all our worldly goods and the smaller white one with our most valued possessions

Flying training for potential military pilots has always been the prerogative of the RAF, but our armed forces have always accepted pilots trained abroad. When we left HMS *St Vincent*, our course was divided into three parts. One went to RAF Sealand in Cheshire, which is now an industrial estate, the second went to RAF Elmdon, which is now Birmingham Airport, and the third went to Pensacola in the United States. Those who stayed in England did their elementary flying training in Tiger Moths while those who went to the US learned on Stearmans. I was sent to RAF Sealand, No 21 EFTS, where my instructor was Sergeant Tate. It was in the month of February and it was really cold. The open cockpits in the Tiger Moth were draughty and we were grateful for the quality of the flying clothing provided.

The communication between the front and rear cockpits was by means of Gosport tubes: our flying helmets were fitted with earpieces and tubes, rather like a doctor's stethoscope (but not actually plugged into the ears) and the 'Y' union where the tube from each ear joined was plugged into one of two larger tubes which connected the two cockpits. The other end of the tube to which the earpieces were connected had a conical rubber mouthpiece which fitted flush to the cheeks and chin (to keep out extraneous noises) while we spoke. It did actually work quite well, but one unexpected disadvantage occurred if either the instructor or the pupil happened to suffer from halitosis.

I thoroughly enjoyed flying the Tiger Moth but I always had difficulty landing it and quite often finished my landing run with a ground loop—luckily, always without damage. This meant that I was the last pilot to go solo and my Chief Flying Instructor's test was left to the last day of the course. It was foul weather—rain, low cloud and blustery, quite strong winds. The CFI was reluctant to carry out a test and the flight kept being postponed until, late in the day, he decided he had to go. Because the wind was so strong and blustery, he decided to taxi out himself and I took off and climbed to just below cloud level. We flew around doing whatever exercises were possible in the conditions until he said, 'Pick a field for a forced landing.' I chose one which looked okay to me so he then closed the throttle and I started my approach to land. However, the wind was so strong that I misjudged it entirely and finished up approaching a rather nice, flat field at least a quarter of a mile from where I thought I was going. At hedge height the CFI took over and said that we would return to base and he would land and taxi back. So ended my CFI check: I was passed fit to continue!

From Sealand we spent a short time in lodgings in Blackpool before embarking for transport to Canada to continue our Service Flying Training. We were delighted to find ourselves at Greenock being taken on board the RMS *Queen Mary*—the biggest ship we had ever seen. Our accommodation was quite comfortable considering that she was being used as a troopship at the time, the cabins which in peacetime would have accommodated two passengers having been modified to sleep ten or more. We were given jobs to do but with so few troops on board for the westward journey they were not arduous and we had plenty of spare time to relax or otherwise enjoy ourselves. The ship steamed at high speed so that U-boats would be most unlikely to be able to attack, even if they had known the intended route, and the voyage was over in five days as we were delivered to New York. What a marvellous sight after three years of blackout back home! The blaze of light and colour was stupendous, but we were not allowed to go ashore to experience it first hand.

Next morning we disembarked on to a train destined for Moncton in New Brunswick, Canada. It was a long, slow journey on wooden slatted seats and so boring that I remember very little about it. Moncton was simply a holding station until the next establishment in the training routine was ready for us. This was No 31 SFTS at Kingston, Ontario, and once again the train journey there was long and tedious although the anticipation of what was ahead buoyed us up.

Once again under RAF control, we were divided into smaller groups and I finished up in No 83 Course with Flying Officer Jones as my instructor on the Harvard II. Compared with the Tiger Moth this aircraft was big and rugged with such modern facilities as a retractable undercarriage, a variable-pitch propeller and air/ground radio (even if it lacked range).

It was in June 1943 when we started flying in Canada. With glorious weather and doing what we had been working towards for months, life could not have been better. We usually flew for half a day and attended ground lessons for the other half, and there were many different ways to spend our off-duty time. The town of Kingston was very pleasant and we were made most welcome by the local people.

There was a station dance every Saturday which was rigorously controlled by the Chief Petty Officer who was the senior naval rating of the RN liaison group of two officers and six ratings under Commander Stringer RN. To bring us all to order, he used to use his Bosun's Call to start the proceedings and to bring them to an abrupt end, but, in between, I thoroughly enjoyed myself. Quite a large number of young ladies were transported from town into the air station for the occasion, and I did find a regular partner who danced beautifully and turned out to be the organist at the Presbyterian Church in town. Being of the same persuasion, I was invited to attend services and lunch at home afterwards. All delightful and all very 'correct'.

Our night flying training was given at Gananoque, a satellite airfield to the east of Kingston in the area known as the 'Thousand Islands' and close to the international bridge to the United States. We usually had a flight during the day prior to night flying and we were warned against trying to fly under the bridge on penalty of being dipped and returned to Britain in disgrace for disobedience. Needless to say, we were all very good boys . . .

The course finished at the end of September, just in time for my nineteenth birthday. There was no such ceremony as a 'Wings Parade' in those days, just a notice saying, 'The following may wear the flying badge . . .'. The thrill of sewing these badges on to our sleeves was really quite emotional.

Our return home was via Halifax, Nova Scotia, on the RMS *Aquitania*—once again, a high-speed dash. We docked at Greenock and then proceeded to Lee-on-Solent, where, yet again, we were divided. We fell in in three ranks outside the Divisional Office. The Divisional Officer opened a window and leant out. He said, 'When I call out your name, fall in in a separate group on the right.' Then he read from a list and eight or ten of our number moved over the right. When this was completed he said, pointing to the larger group, 'You are officers' and to the smaller group on the right, 'You are petty officers. Fall out and collect your travel warrants and uniform allowances from the office.'

So that was it: I was now a Midshipman (A) RNVR and would remain so until my twentieth birthday, nine months hence. To prove it, I wore purple patches on my collar and pilot's wings just below my elbow on my left sleeve.

It was never clear to me what the criterion was for deciding which of us were to be petty officers. Perhaps it was only a coincidence that most of them seemed to have regional accents (not including Scottish or Welsh). It certainly was not intelligence or examination results.

Because there had been a number of fatal accidents among the pilots forming the first of the Barracuda squadrons, Their Lordships had decided in their wisdom that pilots returning from Canada should have extra flying time in monoplanes to prepare them, regardless of the fact that we already had nearly 200 hours dual and solo in monoplanes. This experience was inflicted on us at RAF Errol on the north banks of the Tay between Perth and Dundee. It did one thing for us: we got used to flying at night over blacked-out Britain after our gentle introduction over a very well-illuminated Canada. We flew Master Is and IIs by day and night and added another thirty hours to our total experience. From Errol, we were divided yet again and sent on our various ways for Operational Flying Training—fighters (Seafires), TBR (torpedo-bomber-reconnaissance) biplanes (Swordfish) or TBR monoplanes (Barracudas). I had been selected for TBR monoplanes, and I found myself appointed to RN Air Station Crail (HMS *Jackdaw*).

Below: RNAS Crail in about 1943, with a pair of Barracudas parked in one of the revetments. At this time Crail was home to 785 and 786 Squadrons, both of which were tasked with the training of aircrews in the art of torpedo-bomber-reconnaissance warfare—with the emphasis on torpedo-dropping.

DESIGN AND DEVELOPMENT

Lieutenant-Commander Robert McCandless DSC

THE first of the squadrons operating the Barracuda had various concerns about the aircraft, and it acquired a most unfavourable reputation. It took some time for the problems to be resolved. I came on to the scene somewhat later as a totally inexperienced operational pilot and benefited from the work done by my predecessors. I found the aircraft comfortable, easy to fly and safe. It never let me down in any way during 400 hours of flying it in all weathers. Take-offs were never exuberant, but from my point of view they were safe—and that applied ashore or afloat, day or night, assisted or free. Landings were remarkably steady at all times. I enjoyed flying the aircraft, although it must be said that I did mishandle it on more than one occasion.

The original specification for the aircraft was issued in November 1937 and, with the rate of change of requirements from torpedo-spotter-reconnaissance to torpedo-bomber-reconnaissance to multi-rôle capability, the designers must have had a nightmare. The aircraft was intended to carry the 18-inch, 1,620-pound torpedo and 250 and 500-pound bombs in the bomber rôle. It was to cruise at 186 knots, stay in the air for six hours and have a strike range of 600 miles. It was supposed to weigh not more than 10,500 pounds and to have a British air-cooled engine. There were five contenders for the contract in the beginning, but, with war approaching, the manufacturers found themselves with other commitments and complications and the contract ultimately went to Fairey Aviation. The two designers involved were Marcel Lobelle and Richard Youngman, and they came up with the basic design around the observer's need to carry out Their Lordships' requirements; all else had to be arranged to fit this need.

The engine originally selected by the designers was the Rolls-Royce Boreas/Exe, which had four banks of six cylinders mounted in an 'X' configuration. The engine had been designed and tested satisfactorily in a Fairey Battle airframe. However, Rolls-Royce were having problems with other engines in greater demand at the time, and they were forced to withdraw from further development of the Boreas. This meant, of course, that there was immediate need for a major redesign of the aircraft to fit whichever powerplant was to be available—and the engine selected was going to have to cope with the gradually increasing weight of the aircraft brought about by

Below: P1767, the first Barracuda prototype, in its original configuration with the tailplane set conventionally at the junction of the fuselage and the fin. However, it was found that operating the flaps caused buffeting and severely degraded the effectiveness of the elevators, and so a revision was put in hand.

altered specifications and updated equipment. In the end, the Merlin 30 was chosen, but it was somewhat heavier than the original choice and so there was an immediate need to strengthen the fuselage.

The delays caused by the redesign were exacerbated by the fact that the Merlins were in demand for other high-priority projects, and it was not until December 1940 that the first two prototypes were ready to fly. It was at this stage that the aircraft was given its name—Barracuda.

At this early stage the aircraft had a tailplane similar to that on the Fairey Fulmar, that is, low-level at the base of the fin. The development of the Barracuda from prototype to operational aircraft was not easy because of the occurrence of a number of unrelated problems, for example aircrew being poisoned by exhaust gases, aircraft failing to pull out of dives, wings coming off during manœuvres and aircraft flicking over into a spin while carrying out a steep turn at the bottom of a dive. The remedies for these problems did not come quickly, and for some of them the answers were still being sought even as the first operational squadrons were forming—and still the manufacturers and trials squadrons were having to cope with further alterations and additions to include unplanned Admiralty requirements.

It must have been the urgent need for the aircraft to become operational as soon as possible that lay behind the decision to send the aircraft to 778 Squadron for service trials. These included deck landing trials, which took place on board HMS *Victorious* in May 1941. It was at this time that tail buffeting was being experienced during the landing, and this was caused by the flaps in the landing position causing turbulence over the tailplane and elevators. Thus it was back to the drawing board, with the result that the aircraft were modified to incorporate the high-level tailplane with struts that became one of its recognition features.

An accidental retraction of the undercarriage on the prototype further delayed the trials until October 1941. Subsequent handling trials, including trials with a variety of weapon loads, received favourable opinion, although it was reported that all-up loads of more than 12,820 pounds would cause pilots difficulty in climbing away from a baulked landing. Steep dives such as would be used in torpedo attacks or dive bombing were also thoroughly investigated, and although the nose tended to rise as the speed built up, necessitating the use of the trimmer, generally speaking the aircraft was steady and fully

Below: The same aircraft, now with the tailplane raised some four feet up the fin and braced for rigidity with struts, and clear of any malign influence caused by disturbed air off the flaps.

BARRACUDA

Main image: Barracuda P9667, the first Mk II, showing the early, angled Merlin exhaust system. The prominent 'pins' atop each wing are part of the wing-fold facility: when the aircraft's wings were folded back, they engaged locks located in the outboard leading edges of the tailplane (which can just be made out in this photograph).

controllable in the dive and, at this time, no serious problems were encountered.

Meanwhile pilots at the Aeroplane and Armament Experimental Establishment, Boscombe Down, were becoming concerned about the Barracuda's take-off capability at all-up weights of 13,400 pounds—this was nearly 3,000 pounds greater than the original specification—but worse was to come with yet further changes in requirements, raising the all-up weight to 14,250 pounds and representing, in the pilots' opinions, a step too far.

At about this time the engineers at Fairey Aviation were troubled to find that the first two production aircraft were experiencing buffeting during landing, much the same as had occurred before the modification to the tail unit. None of their attempts to remedy this was successful, and the aircraft were sent to the Royal Aircraft Establishment at Farnborough so that experienced test pilots might investigate the matter and suggest a cure. They made a surprising discovery: it was found that when the pilot's hood was opened for landing there was a disturbed airflow

DESIGN AND DEVELOPMENT

Opposite, bottom: A pristine, factory-fresh, Westland-built Barracuda Mk I—so fresh, indeed, that its serial number and 'Royal Navy' legend have yet to be applied. Despite having received an order for 250 Barracudas, in the event Westland produced only 23.
Below: P9659, a Fairey-built Barracuda Mk I, on pre-delivery flight trials. Notice that only one torpedo crutch is fitted.

over the upper surface of the inboard end of the mainplane and over the tail unit. A redesigned pilot's cockpit and hood did not cure the turbulence, however, and ultimately it was realised that, when the hood was opened, the reduced air pressure on the surface of the mainplane was sucking air out of the interior of the aircraft and that it was this change in the airflow which was causing the problem. The answer was to install an airtight bulkhead between the pilot and observer in order to prevent the low-velocity airflow leaving the cockpit.

Because of the A&AEE's reservations about the aircraft's take-off capability, it was decided that the Merlin 30 (1,260hp) should be replaced by the more powerful Merlin 32 (1,640hp), and the aircraft thus modified became the Barracuda Mk II. There were further trials to decide which propeller would provide the best performance for take-off, and the outcome was the choice of the four-blade Rotol propeller with a diameter of 11 feet 9 inches. Many different exhaust systems were investigated in an attempt to cure the problem of dangerously high

11

Above: A production Barracuda Mk I demonstrates its diving attitude, the massive external flaps at negative incidence. It was vital for pilots to use elevator trim when carrying out this manœuvre, to counteract the aircraft's nose-up tendencies. The prominent leeboards beneath the wing helped to regulate the airflow across the flaps when weapons were carried.

levels of carbon monoxide appearing in the cockpit, before the arrangement of six ejector nozzles on each side proved to be successful while causing the least drag.

By this time, in 1943, two front-line squadrons were equipped with Barracuda IIs, and one aircraft provided by 827 Squadron was being used to investigate a series of fatal accidents that were taking place during normal squadron training for torpedo attacks. In a steep dive using dive brakes, the elevator trim had to be used to counter the marked nose-up changes in trim which occurred when the Youngman flaps were moved to the 'up' position. When the aircraft pulled out of the dive, the flaps were selected to 'neutral' and the elevator trim had to be returned to the straight and level position within two seconds, otherwise the forces on the control column would be greater than the pilot could hold manually. It was considered that failure to adjust the trim in time had caused some of the fatal accidents.

Other accidents, where the aircraft had been seen to flip over during the steep turn (the 'blue turn'*) into the torpedo attack at the bottom of the dive were found to have been caused by sideslip brought on by using too much rudder during the steep turn at high speed. The sideslip effect was that the fuselage blanked off part of the airflow over the tailplane and elevator, giving insufficient control at that critical time. When this was explained to the squadron pilots and it was emphasised that it was essential to use aileron turns without sideslip and to trim back at the right time, the number of accidents was dramatically reduced.

Yet other accidents, where a wing was seen to come off an aircraft during the dive, were ultimately found to be caused by faulty locking pins, exacerbated by the inexorable increase in the weight of the aircraft that caused stresses beyond those taken into account in the designers' calculations. The faulty locking pins were soon replaced, but by this time the squadrons had lost confidence in the machines.

827 Squadron had moved from Lee-on-Solent to Stretton in mid-December 1942, when a number of the Albacore crews were appointed elsewhere and many of the groundcrews were sent to work on the production line at the nearby Ringway factory. Delivery to RNAS Stretton (HMS *Blackcap*) of Barracuda Mk Is to 827 had begun in January 1943, and these were slowly augmented by Mk IIs. During conversion flying, both types were put through demanding manœuvres, and there were no indications of handling problems. The Mk Is were light and pleasant to handle, and both marks would be in contrast to the Mk III with its heavy, bus-like flying qualities.

The Squadron transferred to RNAS Dunino (HMS *Jackdaw II*), a satellite of Crail, on 24 April 1943 and began a torpedo and armament work-up. This was, in fact, the first real trial of the Barracuda in the weapon's rôle. A large number of ALTs (Air Light Torpedo exercises†) were carried out—thirty being typical—but no rogue characteristics had appeared; why no aircraft losses had occurred in the time since delivery of the Barracudas had taken

---

* A 'blue turn' was executed when all the aircraft in a flight turned simultaneously, finishing up in line abreast. A 'red turn' was when the aircraft followed in sequence, turning at the same point as the leader and finishing in line astern.
† Torpedo exercises were categorised as follows: ALT— Attack/Air Light Torpedo; ADT—Attack/Air Dummy Torpedo; ART—Attack/Air Runner Torpedo.

Above: An early production Barracuda Mk II with vacant torpedo crutches and underwing bomb racks. The early, angled exhaust pipes haves been replaced with individual ejector nozzles, but, on the port side at least, the original recess has not been plated over flush with the fuselage. The aircraft's arrester hook is clearly seen in the stowed position.

place, despite so many dives, remains a mystery. Without warning in June 1943, however, the Senior Pilot, who was a competent aviator, dived into the sea during an ALT, and in the space of the next few weeks a total of four aircraft and eleven aircrew were lost. In contrast to actual operations, when aircrew have some idea of the risks involved, the knowledge that more Barracudas would dive into the sea without warning and without hope of recovery was a disturbing thought. No one returned to tell what went wrong, but eyewitness reports suggested that aircraft were flicking into the sea near the bottom of steep dives. Test pilots and Admiralty representatives hastened to Dunino, but no remedial measures were immediately forthcoming. During the period of losses, the Captain of HMS *Jackdaw* (RNAS Crail), who was learning the basics of flying in a Tiger Moth, came to address aircrew at Dunino and informed the audience that they did not know how to fly Barracudas!

Many aircrew were appointed away as a result of these losses, leaving only a handful of pilots to carry on together with their replacements. Lieutenant-Commander Roy Baker-Falkner, a test pilot at the Aeroplane & Armament Experimental Establishment at Boscombe Down who had been involved in the investigations, and who had already visited the Barracuda squadrons to explain problems and their remedies, became CO of 827 Squadron on 12 August 1943 (and ultimately the Wing Leader of the combined squadrons 827 and 830–No 8 TBR Wing). 'B/F' decided that dive brakes would no longer be used and that particular care should be taken to watch turn-and-bank indicators, to ensure that, during a dive, no skid whatsoever should develop. Aileron turns were to be used at the bottom of the dive, and no rudder was to be used in turning on to the target bearing. It was clear that the Barracuda had characteristics that, under certain conditions, could cause catastrophic loss, but 'B/F''s decisions

A Very Clever Design *Commander N. H. Bovey* OBE DSC VRD RNR

The Barracuda II was generally a pleasantly manœuvrable aircraft to fly and to deck land. It was a good weapons platform, and in the hands of well-trained aircrew made an effective contribution from carriers against German warships and merchant-ship convoys. Barracuda squadrons with fighter support put the *Tirpitz* out of action for months, thus removing a significant threat to the D-Day (6 June 1944) build-up.

On the way out to Ceylon in *Victorious* we carried out an ALT on the ship in the Mediterranean which was not well led and resulted in a fairly shallow dive. During this dive I watched the wings of two Barracudas in front of me buckle and collapse, with the inevitable result. One was flown by the Senior Pilot of one of the squadrons and the other by a recently joined pilot. We were all very puzzled by this, but the investigation failed to produce any explanation, so we carried on.

We had no further structural problems in the Far East, but were sent home in December 1944 because the poor overworked Merlin engine lost enough power in tropical conditions to make the aircraft inferior to the Avenger which replaced it.

I went to Crail as an instructor in January 1945 and was there until September. During that time we lost several aircraft during dive-bombing practice, one of which I witnessed and saw it to be a failure similar to that which occurred in the Med. I do not know that aileron turns were practised, but they were a necessary part of the aiming process in dive bombing.

Some years later, I was told that the problem with the Barracuda wings was in the production. The main spar was very heavily stressed and it had been found in some cases that the rivets were not in as straight and parallel a line as they should have been, resulting in overstressing. Whether this is true or not I have no idea, but it seems a reasonable explanation, bearing in mind the fantastic production efforts made by the industry to produce the weapons required.

Structural failure in aircraft is not confined to Barracudas and the numbers were not that high a percentage. A number of accidents occurred to Barracudas owing to mishandling, particularly when lowering the dive brakes when pulling out of a dive—Pilot error? Inadequate training?—and this may have contributed to the bad reputation of the aircraft as accident-prone, but I feel that this is unjustified. As an example of the aircraft's effectiveness and strength, while I was at Crail, a trainee on a night ADT with a dummy torpedo hit the water. The torpedo stove in the base of the aircraft and knocked the air gunner out through the canopy and he was lost. The observer survived with a broken leg, and the pilot flew the aircraft to Crail and landed with over twelve inches missing from each propeller blade.

I think the Barracuda was a very clever design—perhaps a bit too clever. If a more powerful engine had been available, it would have been outstanding—not the Griffon, which was probably still not powerful enough, but possibly the Rolls-Royce Exe which, I believe, was intended. It would then have been able to display its advanced concept of a multi-purpose aircraft with an infinite number of extra bits hung on, which is the way current aircraft are used.

---

on handling techniques eliminated further casualties during diving manœuvres. He was an inspiration to all concerned.

Lieutenant (A) Jeff Gledhill DSC RNZNVR (retiring in the rank of Captain RAN) was another important figure in those early days. He joined 827 Squadron as a sub-lieutenant in 1942 when it was equipped with Albacores. With other 827 pilots, he flew one of the first Mk I aircraft (P9659) and, later, the first Mk II to come off the production line. He was one of about four pilots who flew the Barracuda and took it through its early tribulations to shipborne operations, including those against the German battleship *Tirpitz*, in April–June 1944 and later in deck-landing training.

From time to time comments had been made that attributed the blame for early Barracuda losses to mishandling by pilots accustomed to flying Swordfish and Albacores. Such comments were, according to Captain Gledhill, incorrect and damaging to the reputation of the unfortunate pilots involved. Prior to their acquisition of Barracudas, the pilots of 827 Squadron in the last quarter of 1942 had completed a Fulmar conversion at RNAS Lee-on-Solent on aircraft with a higher wing loading. However, some of the pilots, of whom he was one, had flown Master IIIs at Netheravon or similar aircraft in Canada. One of the pilots killed had spent time on the Barracuda at Boscombe Down. Thus the comment that these pilots were unused to aircraft with higher-wing loading was quite wrong.

In response to a hypercritical article about the Barracuda in a well-known aeronautical journal in 1996 and entitled 'Tested and Failed', Captain Gledhill wrote: 'The Barracuda had many good points but it could hardly be classified as "innocuous", as shown in my letter [published in the FAAOA *News Sheet*, October 1996, Vol. 23, No 2]. Despite several months of demanding squadron flying, there was no indication of catastrophic characteristics whatsoever, until suddenly, during a well-established torpedo attack programme, out-of-control crashes developed. This was not a mishandling problem. Other problems, if my memory serves me correctly, included wings shed (either 827 or 830 Squadron), Machrihanish, 1943 (fatal); fire in cockpit (830 Squadron) during a dive bombing exercise at Muckle Flugga, Shetlands, in December 1943 (fatal); undercarriage collapse during take-off with dummy torpedo, Crail, 1943; one flap up, one down, East Haven, 1944 (fatal); exhaust pipes (Lancaster stubs fitted later). These are just a few random incidents.'

Lieutenant-Commander George Dyke also recalls that period: 'I flew as an observer [on 827 Squadron] in Albacores from 1941 to 1942. (We had a slight brush with the Japanese in the Indian Ocean!) Later that year, in May, I left 827, but I kept in touch. In 1943, when the Squadron was flying Barracudas from the grass field at Dunino, flying was depressingly limited by a series of failures of hydraulic seals, and the undercarriage imposed great strains. Morale dropped badly. At about this time the Squadron started to lose an occasional crew, usually an inexperienced pilot not pulling out of a dive in a torpedo attack. As I recall, no one saw these accidents happen, because the crew lost were in the last aircraft to pull out of the dive.'

The late Lieutenant (A) David A. Brown RNZVR—who served as an observer with 830 Squadron and later became a noted author writing about naval affairs—reported that he received a letter from a former pilot on 827 Squadron in which the latter observed, 'I do not really want to enter the arena by writing an account of things as memory dims, and new facts tend to emerge. I will state that when first appointed to 827 I was "twitched" rigid. Seeing all these aircrew who were discharged, obviously in a bad nervous state, was very off-putting. However, "Daddy B/F" soon sorted everything out and I found the Barracuda a friendly aircraft. It had to be—we survived the war and peace!

'If anything went wrong, it was the high-speed stalling of the wing owing to its high wing-loading when doing a steep V-turn, for example the blue turn in towards the target during an ALT. Unless the ball of the turn-and-bank indicator was in the centre and any slip in evidence, then the aircraft "flipped". This was one thing "B/F" knew from Farnborough and instilled into us unmercifully. That is why we all had to learn to fly the Master or a like single-plane aircraft after leaving Crail and before being let loose on the Barracuda II. (I then went on Lysanders at Arbroath for a few hours before joining 827 at Dunino!)'

Incidentally, in regard to the 'wing-shedding' propensity attributed (mostly in the form of rumours on many occasions) to the Barracuda, Brown, who was at Crail with 711 Squadron at the time, put to the same former pilot the case of three aircraft which, on night ALT exercises over the Firth of Forth during early November 1944, disappeared without trace. So far as Brown was aware, the Naval

Below: Heavy landings frequently resulted in a Barracuda's undercarriage spectacularly collapsing. The identity of this example is not known for certain—although the call-sign on the undercarriage door indicates that the aircraft is from one of the carrier squadrons serving in the Far East at the end of the war and immediately afterwards. Indeed, the 'prang' looks suspiciously similar to that involving 827 Squadron's aircraft depicted on page 124.

Board of Inquiry at Crail did not come to any conclusions about the cause of the disaster, but it was soon widely noised abroad that the Barracudas had all 'shed their wings' in mid-air during the dive and had gone straight into 'the drink'. The pilot's response was that he could not recall ever hearing that three Barracuda IIs had shed their wings at Crail, and moreover, affirmed that, in his lengthy experience with the Barracuda aircraft, he could not remember any such event. 'Anyway, I believe such a statement to be an absolute load of old cobblers. The wings were so solid (witness trying folding and spreading, etc.) and the locking device so robust as to beggar belief.' According to the late Ray Sturtivant, the noted military aviation historian, it appears that, in fact, there were two events, one on 8 November, when 785 Squadron lost two aircraft (LS640 and LS878), and the other on 12 November 1944 when 786 Squadron lost MD762. All three Barracudas failed to return from night exercises, with the loss of three crew members in each case. This revelation makes the 'wing-shedding' theory seem even less plausible than previously thought.

When I joined 827 Squadron in June 1944, the early problems outlined above had been explained and overcome. However, there was still a lot of adverse comment amongst the pilots that rivets were 'popping' on the mainplanes. It was a problem that was never pointed out to me on an aircraft, so I was left wondering. Years later, when I had much more experience in aviation matters—in fact, it was at the time of the Comet disasters, when there was much talk about metal fatigue—I gave a little more thought to the problems of the Barracuda. It occurred to me that this might have been a factor which perhaps had not been understood at the time or had just not been considered.

When we were undergoing dive-bombing training at RNAS East Haven (HMS *Peewit*), we would take off with eight practice bombs and drop these one at a time on the target fairly close to the north bank of the Tay estuary. The Wren range assessors were in two marker positions almost half a mile apart on the beach. Each marker took a bearing on the smoke burst where the 25-pound practice bomb fell, and the point where the bearings crossed fixed the precise position where the bomb landed relative to the target. In this way, the bombing error was recorded for each bomb dropped by each pilot. This meant that each pilot on each sortie was carrying out eight dives. We were intending to dive at an angle of 70 degrees and release as close to the target as possible, probably between 2,000 and 3,000 feet, and then pull out of the dive, and that was when the 'g' forces were really quite high (probably 5 or 6g) and many, if not all, of us partially blacked out for a few seconds.

We then returned to the airfield, where we changed pilots and the aircraft were reloaded with bombs and went off on a repeat sortie. This meant that each aircraft probably carried out at least four sorties a day—that is, 32 dives a day, and with heavy 'g' forces on every one. This could go on for days at a time, and then be repeated for course after course. I could then understand that the training squadron aircraft might well have suffered stress, and this might have been shown by rivets becoming loose or popping. However, aircraft in the front-line squadrons were never exposed to these concentrated spells of maximum 'g', simply because of all the other less strenuous exercises that were carried out.

Throughout this period, development of the Barracuda continued, and it can be assumed that confidence in the aircraft had been established and that it was deemed to be a reliable test-bed for many different modifications. It was about this time, in 1945, that Their Lordships decided to abandon the requirement for the aircraft to carry out torpedo attacks and concentrate on dive bombing.

The rapid rate of improvement in airborne radars caused some quite significant changes. The original radar fitted for the operational squadrons was the metric ASV (Air to Surface Vessel) Mk IIN. This was quite successful in calm seas, but in any sea state above about 3 the radar was reflected by the waves, causing 'snow' all over the observers' screens and rendering nothing distinguishable. The improved version, the centimetric ASV Mk XI,* was fitted to the Barracuda Mk II by removing the aerials from the top surface of the wings and installing an antenna in a ventral blister at the after end of the fuselage, just ahead of the arrester hook. This gave the antenna a clear, uninterrupted scan below the aircraft, and tests proved to be entirely satisfactory. As a result it was decided to fit 25 per cent of the production aircraft with this modification, and Barracudas so equipped were designated Mk III.

Another even more up to-date radar, ASH (Air to Surface Type H), became available at the same time as a modified tailplane was being tested which improved the aircraft's performance in the dive,

---

* Some sources refer to this radar as ASV Mk X. Reportedly, the set was originally designated 'ASVX' (Air to Surface Vessel Experimental), which no doubt explains the inconsistency.

Above: The standard radome position for those few Barracuda IIs fitted with AN/APS-4 was beneath the port wing, as demonstrated here by LS789. The old ASV Mk II yagi aerials atop the wings were of course now redundant, and they were deleted. By this time, too, the value of the airborne torpedo was being questioned; indeed, it was very rarely used in anger by Barracudas.

The photograph offers a clear view of the revised exhaust discharge arrangements for the Merlin engine adopted on the Mk II.
Below: A secret revealed: Barracuda P9645/G, originally a Mk I, modified to carry ASV Mk XI radar, the scanner for which is clearly visible within the clear plastic (Perspex) ventral radome.

reducing the control column forces and even increasing the aircraft's speed while carrying it out. A small number of Barracuda IIs were so fitted, and entered squadron service in this guise, but, more significantly, a more powerful engine became available, the Rolls-Royce Griffon 37 (2,020hp), which allowed a modification to the wing tips, increasing the span and squaring them off. When these were all put together with a modified fin and the ASH radar carried in a pod under the port wing, the aircraft was still recognisably a Barracuda but definitely cosmetically enhanced. This was the Mk V. There is no doubt that it was a much improved aircraft, but the war in the Pacific came to an end and only a handful of this version were built. Another modification fitted to the Mks II and III was the radio altimeter. Unfortunately, the aircrew never really trusted this for night flying, which was its purpose, because of the inconsistencies that had been observed when testing the equipment in daylight.

Above: This ventral Mk XI scanner was adopted for the production Barracuda Mk III, exemplified here by RJ796 serving with 796 Squadron and displayed at the 'Fifty Years of Flying' event at RAF Hendon in 1951. An inert mine is presented on a trestle in front of the aircraft.
Below: The distinction of being the mark of aircraft to which the most tailfin configurations have been fitted must surely belong to the Barracuda V, which enjoyed four differing styles before a fifth was finally decided upon. The original proposal, depicted here by LS479, merely replicated that already featured on the Mk II.
Bottom: At least one of the prototypes, PM940, was fitted with a smoothly executed fillet to the leading edge to its fin, which otherwise remained unchanged from that on earlier marks.

DESIGN AND DEVELOPMENT

Above: RK532 showed a redesigned fin incorporating a severely angular leading edge to the fin fillet but, as on PM940 opposite, retaining the original Barracuda rudder. The Mk V's new Griffon powerplant required a completely redesigned front fuselage, dominated by truly colossal, flame-damping exhaust shrouds. The mark's extended, squared-off wing tips can also be seen in this view, and the absence of underwing leeboards may be noted.
Below: RK535 tested yet another tailfin configuration, retaining the angular leading edge but now featuring a taller, more pointed rudder. All these developments were part of a quest to improve the aircraft's directional stability. Notice the sensor fitted to the starboard wing-lock fairing.
Bottom: Eventually the definitive Mk V emerged, with a fin fillet and an enlarged rudder, now with a rounded tip. Only some thirty Mk Vs were received into the Fleet Air Arm, serving with the second-line 778 and 783 (as here) Squadrons.

19

Missing Its Generation *Commander David Hobbs* MBE

The Fairey Type 100 Barracuda was built in larger numbers than any other British naval aircraft, before or since, and its production involved one of the largest and most complex British industrial projects of its generation. The aircraft that resulted was viewed with critical dislike by many of the aircrew who flew it, while others remember it as an effective weapons platform. Some openly admit to being frightened of it. Good or bad, this complex aircraft should be placed into a fair historical context.

The first Fairey Swordfish TSR squadron was formed in 1936. This aircraft's planned replacement, the equally conservative biplane Fairey Albacore, was ordered into production 'off the drawing board' in May 1937 and flew for the first time in December 1938. Realising that the Albacore would be, at best, only an interim type, the Naval Air Division (NAD) of the Naval Staff informed the Air Ministry on Saturday 29 May 1937 that it required a monoplane torpedo-bomber-reconnaissance (TBR) aircraft to replace it. The Requirement was designated S.24/37. At the time, control of naval aviation was split between the Admiralty, which was responsible for the operational control of embarked aircraft, and the Air Ministry, which was responsible for administrative matters ashore, including the procurement of new aircraft to meet Naval Staff requirements. This flawed and complicated process ended after the Government accepted the findings of a review by Sir Thomas Inskip, the Minister for Defence Co-ordination, in July 1937, which stated, among many other points, that the Admiralty should, by July 1939, regain full control of carrier-borne and other embarked flying, of disembarked shore basing and of the procurement of aircraft for the Royal Navy.

The changeover actually took place in May 1939, but the early stages of Barracuda development fell across this difficult period as the Air Ministry stepped back and the Admiralty was not yet fully ready to take over. It can also be argued that, in the frantic period of rearmament after the Munich Crisis, too much priority was given to the numerical expansion of the Royal Air Force with some fairly 'pedestrian' aircraft types while not enough importance was placed on the Royal Navy's desperate need to develop and manufacture new aircraft. The same period saw big advances in airframe design, with stressed-metal-skinned monoplanes replacing fabric-covered biplanes, but more especially it saw a dramatic growth in engine power. This was typified by the Rolls-Royce Merlin, which offered 1,030hp in 1936 and 1,640hp in 1940.

The officers in the Admiralty's Naval Air Division who drew up the Barracuda's original Staff Requirement clearly wanted an aircraft that represented a radical step forward from the Albacore. They were clearly influenced by the types coming into service with the United States Navy and, perhaps, the Imperial Japanese Navy, both of which services had overtaken the RN in terms of carrier-borne aircraft numbers and capability. The US Navy had initiated the design of monoplane strike aircraft in 1934 and the resulting Douglas TBD Devastator torpedo-bomber and Vought SB2U Vindicator scout/dive-bomber had first flown in 1935 and 1936, respectively. The British would have been well aware that both had taken part in a series of evaluations against equivalent biplanes and had shown marked superiority without any disproportionate inability to operate from a carrier. VT-3, the first TBD-1 unit, formed in October 1937 and VB-3, the first SB2U unit, in January 1938. Intelligence about new Japanese aircraft would not have been as clearly focused, but NAD may have been aware of the Nakajima B5N1 Type 97 'Kate' monoplane torpedo bomber, which first flew in January 1937. The Albacore was thus known to be obsolescent before it had even flown.

Air Ministry conservatism was reinforced by the fact that all Royal Navy pilots were trained by the RAF, making it more difficult for them to take an independent view of future requirements. In November 1936, two years after the US Navy aircraft were specified, the Air Ministry's Operational Requirements Division 2 wrote to the officers in NAD working on the requirement that became S.24/37, stating that 'primary investigation into the design of a dive-bomber/reconnaissance aeroplane has shown that a biplane design must be accepted if features of too experimental a nature are to be avoided.' Fortunately, NAD insisted that it wanted a monoplane. The Fairey Battle, specified in 1932 and the launch customer for the Rolls-Royce Merlin engine, was another possible influence: in service by February 1937, it was already obsolescent by 1939 although it remained in large-scale production in order to keep shadow factories busy.

Unlike the aircraft that influenced NAD's thinking, the RN imposed severe constraints on S.24/37 that would require some ingenuity to overcome. The armoured-deck carriers had small lifts to minimise the size of their unarmoured openings in the flight deck, and the Fairey Type 100, chosen to meet the S.24/37 requirement, had to be designed to fit them. Worse, all naval aircraft were specified to be capable of taking off and landing on the sea with floats and launched from the cradle of a heavy-duty catapult so that they could operate, if necessary, from battleships and cruisers. Whilst this had been reasonable for biplanes, it imposed severe constraints on the new monoplanes that were not pointed out by the Air Ministry, or realised by the Admiralty, until it was too late. Much of the specification concerned the ability of the observer to perform his tasks. The high-mounted wing was to give him the best possible view of the sea surface for reconnaissance and for spotting the fall of shot of the Fleet's guns. The two bulged windows enabled him to see and take bearings over a considerable arc on either beam and almost vertically downwards. The high wing led to a neat design of undercarriage that avoided having to have oleo legs nine feet long but which produced its own complications.

S.24/37 called for the new aircraft to carry a genuine 'ship-killing' weapon, the Mk XIIB torpedo, over a radius of action considerably greater than that of its predecessors. It was also to have the world's first analogue computer-controlled sight so that the weapon could be aimed

Above: Barracuda II MX607—the serial number is marked temporarily on the rear fuselage—takes shape at the Blackburn factory at Brough in Yorkshire. Notice the manner in which the observer's blister window could be opened—a useful facility for him in the event of an emergency. The main oil tank is prominent in front of the pilot's windscreen.

Below: The Merlin engine is installed. The angled channel directing the elongated exhaust pipe of the Barracuda I remained a characteristic of subsequent marks as it was integral to the structure of the forward fuselage, although it was generally plated over prior to finishing. It was only finally eliminated with the re-engined Barracuda V.

BARRACUDA

accurately at its target. By contrast, the TBD-1 had a similar radius of action with a less effective torpedo or a smaller weapon load and the SB2U had about double the radius of action with a 1,000lb bomb. The B5N1, in common with most Japanese naval aircraft, had a considerably greater radius of action.

The Barracuda was inevitably to be a big, complicated aircraft, and the key to its ability to meet the required performance was its engine. The original selection was the remarkable Rolls-Royce Exe (the first RR engine to be named after a river). This powerplant was conceived in 1936 as a very advanced 24-cylinder, 90-degree, X-shaped engine similar in concept to the Vulture that eventually powered the Avro Manchester. It was a pressure-air-cooled, sleeve-valve engine which was lighter than the more conventional Merlin without its need for coolant fluid, radiators and 'plumbing' and which would have delivered 1,200hp initially. It also had a significantly lower drag factor. A development Exe was fitted in a Fairey Battle testbed that proved to be so trouble-free that it was used by Fairey as a hack transport until 1943, long after the engine development had been curtailed; it was also faster than Merlin-powered Battles.

The first major setback to Barracuda development came in 1939 when Rolls-Royce terminated work on the Exe in line with Government policy to concentrate on Merlin development and production. (Surprisingly, the less advanced but equally high-technology Vulture was kept in development for the Manchester bomber, thereby demonstrating the relative priorities apportioned by the Ministry of Aircraft Production.) The Bristol Taurus and the American Wright Cyclone air-cooled radial engines were both considered as replacements but neither ran on 100-octane fuel and, thus, both were considered to lack not only the high performance but also the development potential required for the new TBR. Valve improvements to the Merlin to allow it to run on 100-octane fuel were in hand and the Barracuda was redesigned to take the Merlin 30, delivering 1,300hp below 6,000 feet at 3,000rpm and +12.5 pounds boost. It was designed for use in RN aircraft but was significantly heavier and had a greater drag factor than the Exe, both of which characteristics limited the Barracuda's performance.

A second blow came in the summer of 1940 after the fall of France, when priority was given to fighter production by the MAP and work on the Barracuda prototype was halted. By the time this aircraft flew, in August 1942, the rôle of naval aviation had expanded enormously and new aircraft needed to be fitted with radar, improved communications, an array of new weapons and the strengthened airframe and wings to carry them. The designed all-up weight had increased from 10,500 to 14,250 pounds, decreasing the performance and increasing stresses on the aircraft structure. Effectively, the Barracuda had missed its generation and the contemporaries against which S.24/37 had been drawn up over five years earlier were already being replaced in the US Navy by the magnificent Grumman Avenger with which the Barracuda is inevitably compared.

The Avenger was specified in April 1940 when the US Navy was able to take advantage of the British wartime

Opposite page: The propeller installation on a production Barracuda Mk II. Above: The ill-fated Rolls-Royce Exe powerplant.

experience which had been passed on to it. The 1,700hp Wright R-2600-8 Cyclone engine took full advantage of the advances in engine technology that preceded this aircraft's design and the US Navy had been involved closely in its development. The engine had sufficient power to maintain good performance in the hot conditions found in the Pacific whereas the Merlin of the Barracuda did not. It came as no surprise, therefore, that when sufficient Lend-Lease Avengers became available in 1944 they replaced Barracudas in the strike squadrons of the British Pacific Fleet.

In summary, the Barracuda was a radical aircraft that missed its generation because, at a time of rapid technological advance, the British Government failed to understand the Royal Navy's critical and legitimate need for new aircraft. The MAP, designed to streamline aircraft production, had the opposite effect and in reality blocked the Barracuda's entry into service by nearly three years; had it come into service in 1940 instead of 1943 it could have been the right aircraft in the right place. When it did arrive in the Royal Navy's front-line squadrons, it was not the aircraft they needed and it was too late.

FROM THE COCKPIT

Lieutenant-Commander Robert McCandless DSC

MY first impression of a Barracuda was that it was an ungainly looking machine, and I suppose that this was mainly because of the unusual undercarriage. The design was unusual because the aircraft was a high-wing monoplane: the mainplanes were attached at the 'shoulders' of the fuselage and the undercarriage was required to retract into the underside of the mainplane. The length of the undercarriage legs and the distance between the wheels were imposed on the designers by the need to have sufficient clearance for a torpedo on its trolley to be run underneath the fuselage for loading on to the aircraft and space for the torpedo men to work around it.

The designer's answer to these requirements was to make the legs in the shape of an inverted 'L'. The crossbar of the 'L' was hinged at its point to the bottom of the fuselage and the upright of the 'L' was the actual oleo leg down to the wheel. The 'L' was supported and held in the 'down' position by a strut which connected the top of the oleo leg and the underside of the mainplane. When the undercarriage retracted, the strut, which was hinged in the middle, folded and the crossbar of the 'L' retracted into the fuselage while the oleo and wheel retracted into the underside of the mainplane. As with all the Fleet Air Arm aircraft of the time, there was a tail wheel which was non-steerable and did not retract. In the air, the Barracuda looked very much better.

Another unusual features was the Youngman flaps. These were separate aerofoils about eight feet long and two feet wide, and each was attached by two hinges to the inboard end of the trailing edge of the mainplane and set about nine inches below. They could be lowered to an angle selected by the pilot for take-off and fully down for landing. They could also be raised to one fixed position, when they became air brakes (more usually referred to as 'dive brakes'). A third feature was that the tailplane and elevators were set very high on the fin because, when the flaps or air brakes were used, the turbulence caused would have reduced the effectiveness of the elevators to a dangerous extent if they had been attached to the base of the fin.

Along the top of the fuselage was a Perspex 'greenhouse' covering all three crew members—pilot, observer and TAG (Telegraphist Air Gunner). The hood of the pilot's cockpit slid back on runners and was very easy to operate. Above the observer's position was another sliding section giving him access, and at the after end was a section which was hinged in such a way that as well as giving the TAG access (made initially via a retractable footstep in the fuselage) allowed him to deploy his guns for action while shielding him from the slipstream. Generally speaking, the TAG was discouraged from opening his hood in circumstances where the guns were not

Left: Its massive, angular undercarriage, looking for all the world like so much scaffolding, gave the Barracuda a very ungainly appearance when the aircraft was at rest. This particular machine, DP855/G, was an early Mk II (with a three-bladed propeller) modified to serve as the prototype Mk III, the chief distinguishing feature of which was the new ventral radome which can just be glimpsed aft.

Below: Detail of a crashed Barracuda undergoing inspection at RNAS Portland, revealing the Merlin engine and also some of the intricacies attending the cockpit canopy, including the triangular deflector panels attached to the windshield framework (a measure of draughtproofing that was surely welcome to the pilot, seated as he was only a couple of feet from the wing-root leading edges). Both the pilot's and the observer's hoods have been slid back here, and the observer's wind deflector is in the raised position. The angled post in the centre of the upper surface of the wing is a stub strut to help secure the wing when it was folded (as shown in the upper photograph on page 26); the small angled strut at the inboard leading edge is a retractable handgrip to assist the clamber up to the pilot's and observer's cockpits.

Above: Barracuda II–MD771–'E1E' here, though clearly carrying different markings not long before this photograph was taken–in the hangar of the escort carrier HMS *Battler* in summer 1945, folded, chocked and stowed to minimise the amount of space it occupies. The aircraft is from 767 Squadron, the deck landing training unit normally based at RNAS East Haven.
Below: A 769 NAS Barracuda Mk II, based at RNAS Rattray, with the aircrew's 'greenhouse' configured for maximum ventilation, including, unusually, the hinged portion of the observer's hood in the open position.

The Naval Air Fighting Development Unit, however, in their report of May 1943, noted that 'On one occasion when the [observer's] gun was being tested [the midship wind deflector hood] was pulled open to allow the observer to man his gun. Almost immediately the retaining catch worked loose and the hood was slammed down by the slipstream, striking the observer on the head. This very temporarily rendered him unconscious.' Notice the first character of this aircraft's fuseage code–a lower-case 'i', emphasising the fact that it is a letter, not a numeral.

required to be deployed because, while the hood was protecting the TAG, it was causing turbulence which adversely affected the efficiency of the elevators and rudder. It was particularly discouraged during landing. On each side of the fuselage, beneath the mainplanes, was a blister window some three feet by two feet in size for the observer's cockpit.

Standing on the upper surface of the mainplanes, fairly close to the tips, were the aerials for the ASV radar. These were quite sturdy pieces of equipment and I always wondered how much drag they caused. The pins for securing the mainplanes when they were folded were also prominent on the upper surface of the wings out near the tips.

When the wings were folded, there was a section of the mainplanes, about eight feet by three feet of the trailing edge at the inboard end, to which the Youngman flaps were attached, which folded upwards, hinged on the main spar and hydraulically operated by the ground crew. This folded well over on to the upper surface of the mainplane to give clearance for the whole mainplane to be swung backwards manually. It was hinged on the main spar, and secured to a spring clip on the tip of the tailplane. It was secured by means of a rod which was permanently fitted to the upper surface of the mainplane—yet more drag! For manual wing folding and spreading there was a triangular handle, normally recessed in the underside of the mainplane near the wing tip. These were lowered by the pilot and were large enough to allow two or three ratings to move the wings safely, even in strong windy conditions. The wings were locked in the spread position by means of a substantial locking pin which was operated manually by a member of the groundcrew.

On the Barracuda I, the engine exhaust was taken by means of a fairly large pipe, usually referred to as the 'stovepipe', from the top of the engine, angled down the side of the fuselage to a point below the horizontal datum of the observer's cockpit. This was changed during Mk II production to a system of ejector exhaust stubs, in the interests of engine efficiency and drag reduction. Night flying pilots of the time were less impressed because the hot gases of the exhaust could give them a somewhat distorted view of the DLCO (Deck Landing Control Officer, or 'batsman') when landing on board a carrier. However, we all got used to it.

The pilot's cockpit could not be described as spacious, but it was not constricted for someone of average size and weight. There was a bucket seat, and the pilot sat on his folded parachute and emergency dinghy. The seat could be raised and lowered only and the rudder pedals could be adjusted according to need. The parachute harness was, of course, fitted first, making sure that the dinghy lanyard was attached by quick release to the 'Mae West' lifejacket. The four seat straps were then fitted, two coming up from the sides of the 'bucket' and two coming down from strong points above the shoulders. All four were fastened in the centre with a single pin held in position by a quick-release clip. This simple arrangement was well designed and worked very successfully, as I proved entirely to my own satisfaction. The pilot plugged his radio connection into a socket fixed to the seat between his legs. The back of the seat was very nearly vertical and it might have been just a little bit more comfortable had it been raked back a few more degrees.

The control column was standard for that time, simply a straight tube and a spade grip with a weapon release button on it and a short lever for operating the hydraulic brakes. The hydraulic power was distributed differentially between the brakes on the main wheels by moving the rudder bar, a full left rudder gave full braking on the port wheel, leaving the starboard wheel to run free; the opposite result was achieved by applying full starboard brake. Both main wheels braked equally when the rudder bar was central. The hand lever was applied when the rudder was in the desired position and it could be locked in the central position for parking. The tail wheel was not steerable, so taxying was controlled entirely by differential braking on the main wheels.

Because of the tail-down attitude of the aircraft on the ground, and the fairly long nose of the engine, it was essential to swing the nose from side to side when taxying, to make sure that the way ahead was clear. If it was required to make a tight turn, it was necessary to put on full rudder, apply the brake lever and open the throttle to increase the slipstream across the rudder, which was, of course, fully over to the side and in position to assist by pushing the tail round. I considered the aircraft easy to handle on the ground, ashore or afloat. Taxying with the wings folded was kept to an absolute minimum on board and forbidden ashore.

The throttle quadrant on the port side of the cockpit was standard for the time. The throttle itself

Below: Another view of the crashed Barracuda at Portland (see page 25), permitting here a glimpse into the front cockpit and showing some details of the pilot's headrest and seat harness. Notice, too, the substantial grab handles (interior locking releases) for moving the canopy along its slide rails. The vents immediately forward of the windscreen allowed hot air to be released for de-icing.

was a straight lever with a RATOG (Rocket Assisted Take-Off Gear) firing button on top. Alongside it was the propeller pitch control lever. Both could be held firmly in position by tightening a knob which clamped both levers at their hinges. This was always used to the full during catapult launches. Directly ahead of the throttle quadrant there was a small knob protruding from the instrument panel. This controlled a manifold inlet pressure override and was usually referred to as 'the booster tit'. When it was pulled, it was locked in this position with a spring clip and the manifold inlet pressure increased to +18 pounds of boost.

Immediately aft of the throttle quadrant, and at about the level of the bucket seat, was the elevator trim. This was a wheel about six inches in diameter, with a knob which allowed the wheel to be wound quickly either forward (clockwise/nose down) or backward (anti-clockwise/nose up). This control moved a small section of the trailing edge of the elevator up or down, giving lift at that point and helping the pilot to move the whole elevator or to trim the aircraft to fly straight and level with no vertical forces on the control column.

Fitted on a shelf above the trim controls was an unusual instrument, namely the Torpedo Control. This was a metal disc about four inches in diameter with a circle printed on it which was divided into 360 degrees, with 0 degrees aft and 180 forward; '0 degrees' represented the heading of the target ship on a steady course. Mounted in the centre of the circle was a large switch shaped like a ship with a sharp end and a blunt end. This switch could be turned though 360 degrees and was connected directly to the controls within the torpedo. We could set the estimated ship's speed on the control, and there was another switch that could be moved from side to side and marked 'Avoiding', 'Away' or 'Towards'.

Below the elevator trim was the rudder trim. This was a knurled wheel about three inches in diameter fitted horizontally in a small alcove just big enough to allow a gloved hand to fit over the wheel and to move it easily. The wheel operated in the natural

Below: Detail of the Barracuda II pilot's main instrument panel (although the vertical speed indicator is missing from the 'standard panel' and an extra compass has been attached, in somewhat Heath Robinson fashion). The brake lever is prominent, behind the control column handgrip, and the pilot's Gosport tube may be seen clipped across the top of the panel.

sense in that if it was turned to the left (anticlockwise) the nose of the aircraft turned marginally to the left and if to the right (clockwise) it turned to the right). This trim tab operated in exactly the same way as the elevator trim, not so much helping the pilot to move the rudder as keeping the aircraft on a steady heading without having to keep any weight on the rudder bar. Both of these trim tabs were of considerable assistance in maintaining straight and level flight, which was so important to the accurate flying required for navigation—and absolutely essential when flying out of sight of one's carrier base, over featureless seas, perhaps in poor visibility and maintaining radio silence (there was no satnav in those days!). Of course, because we were returning to a moving base, the observer was briefed before take-off about the ship's intended course and speed, but the intentions were not always followed.

The ailerons also had trim tabs, but these could not be adjusted from the cockpit. If a pilot found that an aircraft was flying one wing low to the extent that he had to hold it up with the control column to maintain straight and level flight, he would report it to the aircraft's ground crew and the trim tab would be adjusted by hand and the next pilot to fly the plane would be asked specifically to report on the trim when he returned.

On the floor beside the pilot's seat was a 'hammer head' handle which was the release for the RATOG equipment after firing. Below the throttle quadrant were the controls for lowering the deck hook, selecting undercarriage up and down and for selecting one of four positions of the Youngman flaps. When the flaps were in the normal position for flying, the lever was in a gated position in the centre. The lever was moved upward to select the dive brakes and downward to select flaps for take-off and landing. For take-off an intermediate position of 15 or 20 degrees could be selected by moving the lever down to 'Landing' and then moving it back to 'Neutral', when the required selection showed on the flap position indicator on the forward instrument panel directly above the lever. The flaps were, of course, selected fully down for landing.

There were no forward firing guns in the Barracuda (although a single, wing-mounted Browning was carried by the later Mk V) and there was no gun sight to help with aiming, so dive bombing and depth charge dropping were very much a matter of guesswork modified by experience. However, by 1945 a dive bombing sight had been devised, but it was being fitted to aircraft just in time for the end of the war and thus none of the front-line aircraft being sent out to the Pacific were able to use the equipment either in practice or in anger.

In the centre of the instrument panel were the six flight instruments, namely the airspeed indicator (air pressure from the pitot head), the artificial horizon (gyro), the climb and descent indicator (operated by measuring the rate of change of barometric pressure), the altimeter (barometric pressure with control to set local reading before landing), the directional gyro (with control in order to synchronise with the magnetic compass) and the turn-and-slip indicator (turn measured by gyro and slip by movement of a black ball by gravity in a semi-circular tube like an inverted spirit level).

Immediately below the panel of flight instruments were a number of knobs, switches and instruments including the automatic boost control cut-out (the 'tit'), the engine slow running cut-out, the DR compass and switches, the fuel pressure warning light, the fuel cock (which controlled the flow of fuel from the various tanks), the handling rails release,

Below: The wartime Barracudas lacked a sighting device but the Naval Air Fighting Development Unit (787 Squadron) at RAF Wittering carried out trials with a gyro gun sight, see here fitted in one of its aircraft. However, it arrived in service too late to be utilised effectively in action.

the undercarriage warning lights and the magnetic compass.

To the port side of the panel were more instruments: the radio altimeter, the cylinder priming pump, a further undercarriage warning light, the flaps position indicator, ignition switches, the radio altimeter indicator lights ('traffic lights'), the landing lamp direction control and switch, the air intake heat control and the air temperature gauge. To the starboard side of the panel were the windscreen de-icing pump, the pressure head (pitot) heater switch, the engine rpm gauge, the inlet manifold pressure gauge (boost), the radiator temperature gauge, the oil pressure gauge, the oil temperature gauge, two fuel contents gauges, the starter re-loading control, the engine starter switch, and switches for the recognition lights, navigation lights, formation lights and downward recognition lights switch and, at low level, the F.46 camera switch. On the starboard side of the cockpit were the bomb selection panel with the master switch immediately below, the torpedo selection panel, the oxygen regulator and light switches, the undercarriage emergency lowering gear, the radio altimeter setting switch, the radiator shutter control, the radiator shutter position indicator, the navigation lights dimmer switch, the sixteen-point bomb distributor box and the fire extinguisher. Adjacent to the bucket seat was the seat height adjusting lever.

Below: A close view of a Barracuda II amidships, showing the characteristic 'greenhouse' covering all three crew members, the vast, semi-detached Youngman flap for the port wing, and the offset main aerial mast.

The Pilot's Notes issued in 1944 show pictures of the intercom between pilots, observer and Telegraphist Air Gunner (TAG) by means of Gosport tubes and give no indication of radio equipment, transmit button or switch, channel selection or IFF, but my memory does not bring Gosport tubes to mind at all. I can only assume that radio modifications were fitted at some time fairly soon after the Pilot's Notes were printed because all the Barracudas I flew had radios.

The design requirements for the Barracuda were being produced in 1937, so it should be borne in mind that there were no aviators in the upper echelons of the Admiralty. The main armament was in the big guns of the battleships and cruisers, so obviously the opinions of the gunnery officers were of prime importance.

Since warships had first been built, their captains and admirals were always keen to expand their horizons—hence the 'crow's nest' as high up the masts as was feasible. As soon as other ways of getting men into the air were shown to be possible, they took a keen interest, and, as a result, balloons and airships were investigated. Thus was born the famous maxim 'Find, fix and strike': 'find' by having an observer positioned at as great a height as possible so as to have the widest view, so that the Admiral could deploy his fleet and perhaps obtain an advantage; 'fix' by giving the gunnery direction officers the bearing and estimated distance of the targets; and 'strike' by spotting the fall of shot at the most effective range and, ideally, beyond the range of the enemy.

Of course, during World War II, with the development of the use of aircraft, the 'Find, fix and strike' dictum evolved as well: 'find' involved a search by aircraft over as wide an area of sea as possible, so far as the weather and the endurance of the aircraft would permit; 'fix' was achieved by 'dead reckoning' navigation during the search, whereupon the observer could calculate the position of the target and pass this to the TAG, who would send a W/T message back to the Senior Officer of the Strike Force; and 'strike' meant that, having received the W/T message giving the position of the target, a description of the target (for example, its size and composition) and its present course and estimated speed, the Senior Officer could make the necessary tactical decisions, the reporting aircraft continuing to shadow the target as long as his endurance would allow or until a replacement could release him. The hunting and destruction of the German battleship *Bismarck* in May 1941 is the classic illustration of the principle.

Thus all naval aircraft—other than the single-seat, short-range fighters—in the early days were designed to transport an observer to a position where he could best meet the requirements of the gunnery officers. The development of the aircraft to be the primary weapon system and the changes of opinion in the higher echelons were slow to develop. It is not the intention here to give a history of this development but merely to give a background to the design requirement of the observer's position in the aircraft. Simply put, he had to have the best seat in the house.

The blister windows were designed to give the observer 360 degrees of vision ahead to astern and vertically downwards, and this he was able to facilitate from his seated position on the floor of the cockpit. This position was comfortable and there was well-designed stowage for all the equipment he was required to use in his navigational duties as well as his searching to 'find, fix and strike', plus, of course, a convenient place for his parachute. If he stood up, he could have 340 degrees of vision horizontally,

Right: One of the early production Barracuda Is retained for testing purposes (hence the 'P'-for-prototype marking), P9647 is seen here fitted with an external fuel tank. This side view also clearly shows the observer's blister window located either side of the fuselage, beneath the wing root; further aft, and partially obscured by the Youngman flap, are the windows for the TAG. The use of orthochromatic film for this photograph has turned the yellow-coloured components of the fuselage markings virtually black.

Above: A Barracuda III of 744 Squadron flying with the observer's hood raised. However, in the immediate postwar years, when this photograph was taken, 744 NAS was an anti-submarine training unit and the observer's station was frequently occupied by instructor pilots. The Barracuda's characteristic dinghy release lanyard, running across the port side of the rear fuselage, has been secured by means of patches of fabric in the usual way, and this one follows the route often favoured later in the aircraft's career.

with a small blind spot forward where the pilot's head was in his line of sight. Upwards, his view was totally unrestricted.

Both blister windows had a magnetic compass fitted to them so that the observer could quickly take bearings, for example during wind-finding or during navigational position or target position fixing. Both windows had hinges at the top edges which allowed them to open fully. This facility was not only useful on the ground but also gave the observer a very convenient and quick escape route, if required, when the aircraft was flying.

There was a small hole some six inches in diameter in the bulkhead between the pilot and observer at about the level of the pilot's waist. I always assumed that this was intended to allow the observer to pass a written instruction or some other important object to the pilot. I only ever tried it once with my observer. It was relatively easy for me, but the observer would have needed an extension on his arm to be able to reach the hole!

The observer could strap into his seat in the normal way, and that was certainly required during torpedo- or dive-bombing attacks as well as during fighter-evasion 'corkscrewing'. However, if he was required to stand up, perhaps for hand photography out of the open hood (or, in the very early days, for manning his machine gun if such were present), he had a 'dog lead' which attached to his harness between his legs, giving him freedom of movement as far as the confines of the cockpit were concerned yet making sure he remained within the aircraft if there were any unexpected negative 'g'.

Lieutenant David Brown (see page 15), who was an observer on Barracudas over a period of some twenty-one months (1943–44), including twelve months' operational service with No 8 Naval TBR Wing on board HMS *Furious*, *Formidable* and *Indefatigable*, and had previously trained on Proctors, Swordfish, Albacores and Walruses, said that he could 'only express the greatest praise for the Barracuda from the observer's aspect, and I believe, from the Telegraphist Air Gunner's point of view also. It is true that the observer had very little view directly forward apart from the two side, bulged square ports, but navigation and communication under flight conditions were well catered for.'

The Telegraphist Air Gunner's cockpit was at the back end of the 'greenhouse'. He climbed into the cockpit up the side of the fuselage via a retracting step in the bottom of the fuselage and two spring-loaded flaps which opened inwards to give hand and foot holds and then closed to give a smooth skin without holes. His hood opened from the rear under the action of springs, and then it had to be pulled down to close it with a locking handle. The swivelling bucket seat normally faced aft, and there were two windows at about waist level which were intended to give some degree of downward view. These were not very successful and ultimately they were often faired over. The TAG sat on his parachute. The two 0.303-inch machine guns were stowed aft of the cockpit under a sliding cover and there was accommodation for five drums of ammunition. My own TAG felt that these latter could have been more secure, because on one occasion a drum came loose during some violent manoeuvering—and these objects were rather heavy to be flying around in the cockpit!

The TAG's cockpit also contained smoke floats and flame floats, used as markers and launched down a chute at the TAG's feet. Because of the need for accurate navigation, the observers needed to carry out a wind-finding manoeuvre on every sortie

Below: Two Wrens and a matelot pose for a publicity photograph with a 798 Squadron early-production Barracuda Mk II at RNAS Lee-on-Solent. Notice the substantial 'Undercarriage Locked' reminder disc hanging from the main undercarriage well, the associated pin needing to be removed before flight.

Above: An experimental Vickers machine gun installation in one of the Barracudas assigned to the NAFDU. As can be seen, the field of fire was somewhat restricted—there was precious little scope forward of the beam and not much more below the horizontal.

out of sight of the ship, and these were the markers used for that purpose regularly as well as on other less frequent occasions.

In 1944 the Barracuda was fitted with a TR.1115 W/T set, transmitting Morse code. There was stowage for frequency coils, a very cumbersome method of changing frequencies, and a reel containing a long wire aerial with lead weights on the end. The pilot had to be told when the aerial was in use so that he would not fly too low and possibly do serious damage by, or lose, the aerial. There was also stowage for a Very pistol and the different coloured cartridges which were needed for signalling according to a prearranged code. The pistol was fired out of the open hood.

My TAG (Leading Airman Ron Hibbs) was, like myself, of average height and build and he found the cockpit comfortable and convenient to operate, but he had colleagues who were larger and bulkier and who, if they were wearing Irvine jackets, found it all a bit snug. He thought it was easy to leave the aircraft, and during any of the more exciting occasions, such as dive bombing or deck landing, he always sat facing aft with his hand on the hood release! He said that he enjoyed those activities!

We practised one very violent exercise called fighter evasion. The aircraft formation would open out to quite a wide position, but still aiming to keep the leader in view, and then, on the TAG's instruction 'Stand by to corkscrew. Go!', we would begin the manœuvre. The Barracuda was put into a vicious dive, away from the other aircraft in the formation, requiring the use of both hands on the control column plus full rudder. As soon as we were going down we pulled back up the other way with full aileron and full opposite rudder, then immediately reversed again, keeping this going until the fighter had—it was hoped—overshot.

I do not know of any TAGs who fired their guns in anger from a Barracuda, although some may have done so during the attacks on Japanese installations in the Far East. For our part, the only live firings I personally know of were carried out at Loch Eriboll, near Cape Wrath (during the practice before the attacks on the German battleship *Tirpitz*), and in the course of an exercise in the North African desert near El Alamein.

The TAG had the most restricted view from the aircraft. His view forward of the mainplane was completely blocked and the after end of the fuselage and tailplane restricted the view in that direction. So his clear arc was about 45 degrees below the horizontal from the tip of the mainplane round to the tip of the tailplane and upwards from directly above his head down to the tailplane. Nevertheless, his view in those directions was essential during anti-submarine or other searches and for protection against enemy fighters.

BARRACUDA

Nothing If Not Unprepossessing *Captain Eric Brown* CBE DSC AFC

The Swordfish, so the records say, was responsible for the sinking of a greater tonnage of enemy shipping during World War II than most other Allied aircraft. There is no gainsaying the records, but such success attributed to a relic of an era long past—the Swordfish was assuredly an anachronism long before Adolf Hitler cast covetous glances in the direction of Poland—is difficult to reconcile today with such total obsolescence. Its intended successor, the Albacore, was hardly the advance the Navy's aircrew had a right to expect, being, as was suggested at the time of its debut, no more than a 'tarted up Swordfish', offering its crew reasonable means of answering one of the calls of nature and less likely to encourage pneumonia. Romantic of appearance through these bestrutted and braced biplanes were to some, evoking nostalgia, as they did, for the days when the tempo of aeronautical development was more leisurely, they must surely have had any Luftwaffe fighter pilot that encountered them rubbing his eyes in disbelief.

Inevitably, therefore, the TSR (torpedo-spotter-reconnaissance) boys awaited with bated breath the arrival of the long-promised and much-vaunted monoplane that sported the highly emotive appellation of Barracuda and promised to enable them to vault the decade or so between the concept of their antiquated and supremely vulnerable biplanes and the early 1940s. I assume that they were to be just as astonished as I was at first sight of the monster that was in due course to materialise as the fulfilment of their anticipation. Could this really have been spawned by Marcel Lobelle's drawing boards, where such aesthetically appealing creations as the delectable little Fantôme and pleasingly handsome if somewhat ineffectual Fulmar had seen birth?

I was serving with the Service Trials Unit at Arbroath in September 1942, when our first Barracuda arrived. As it entered the airfield circuit, it could he seen that its contours were nothing if not unprepossessing. Here were no rakish lines such as those of its namesake, that voracious West Indian fish. Then it turned on to the approach and disgorged a mass of ironmongery from wings and fuselage,

Right: As a test pilot evaluating the Barracuda, the writer was generally unimpressed, but he concedes that its deck landing capabilities were excellent. As this photograph of a 767 Squadron Barracuda just about to take the wire on board HMS *Battler* shows, the airframe offered a good deal by way of lift and drag to aid the pilot in his approach.

transforming the pedestrian and unappealing into what could only be described as an airborne disaster. The old adage, 'If it looks right . . .', inevitably sprang to mind, and I concluded that there were events that I could await with rather more pleasure than taking this quaint contraption into the air.

A high-shoulder-wing, all-metal, stressed-skin monoplane, the Barracuda was something of an abortion on the ground. Indeed, with everything folded it gave the impression of having been involved in a very nasty accident. Its most distinctive feature was provided by the Fairey-Youngman flaps—effectively separate aerofoil surfaces mounted inboard of the ailerons and below and behind the wing trailing edge which were lowered some 20 degrees to increase take-off lift and about 30 degrees for fast descents. When in neutral they merely augmented the wing area. The strut-braced, high-set tailplane was another curiosity of the Barracuda, this feature having been adopted when it had been ascertained during prototype trials that the wake from the flaps buffeted a normally positioned tailplane (i.e., one positioned at the junction of fuselage and vertical surfaces). Yet a further unorthodox feature of the aircraft was the design of its mighty undercarriage. The main legs were inverted L-shaped assemblies pivoted near to the base of the fuselage and raised or lowered by jack struts attached at the elbows, the base of each inverted 'L' assembly retracting, complete with fairing, into the fuselage side and the remaining portion of the leg with wheel and fairing retracting into a wing well.

All in all, this large and relatively heavily loaded aeroplane appeared to call for a degree of circumspection, a view that remained with me when, a few days after the arrival of Barracuda Mk I P9645, the fourth production example, I clambered into the cockpit for an initial air test and for what was to be my second experience of an underpowered aircraft, the first having been the Blackburn Roc. The Barracuda had been conceived for the 1,200hp Rolls-Royce Exe 24-cylinder, X-type, pressure-air-cooled, sleeve-valve engine, but further work on this powerplant had been halted and the initial production Barracuda had been provided with a Merlin 30 of 1,300hp —eight per cent more power than originally envisaged but hardly commensurate with the weight that had meanwhile been taken on. The result was that the Merlin and the three-bladed Rotol propeller that it drove provided a woefully insufficient combination to lift off the Barracuda in anything like a reasonable distance, and take-off was to prove a nail-biting business on Arbroath's short runways.

After what seemed an eternity, this monstrosity eventually unstuck and the anxiety of parting company with a rapidly diminishing portion of runway gave place to a few perspiration-evoking moments until those gangling undercarriage legs laboriously tucked themselves out of sight. Matters then began to improve, but the rate of climb was

Opposite, bottom: An early-production Barracuda Mk I similar to that which the writer first took aloft, in September 1942 at RNAS Arbroath.
Below: A Blackburn-built Barracuda Mk II, clearly showing the positions of the underwing bomb racks. The early-style exhaust pipe is still evident.

anything but inspiring and I could not help wondering what effect on climb would result from a torpedo being slung underneath. Once cruise altitude had been reached, I found that the Barracuda was quite pleasantly manœuvrable, being particularly light on the ailerons but displaying a mild suspicion of rudder overbalance. Surprisingly, it revealed a good turn of speed in diving—a characteristic certain to be appreciated by the TSR boys, whose survival often depended on a fast descent from cruise level to sea level to reduce vulnerability to ships' flak and fighter defences. Equally important with fast dive capability was, of course, the ability to dive steeply to give maximum deflection angle changes to the opposing anti-aircraft guns. Both Swordfish and Albacore could dive steeply, but with little acceleration. On the other hand, a monoplane offered the diving speed, but angle could not be steep if pull-out at low level was to be effected safely, a problem that Marcel Lobelle and his team had not-so-neatly solved by means of the previously mentioned Fairey-Youngman flaps. During my initial flight I made only a perfunctory check of these flaps, which seemed very effective, but I was to make much closer acquaintance with them later on the Barracuda II.

When it came to landing—and particularly deck landing—the Barracuda's characteristics were the exact antithesis of those that it displayed as it struggled to get airborne. In short, while take-off could only be described as very poor, the landing could be said to be very good. With everything down, there was so much drag that the Merlin 30 demanded about +4 pounds boost on the approach, and when the throttle was cut at the *moment critique* the Barracuda sank like a stone and remained glued on the deck. The view from the cockpit for this process was good.

I was destined to have little to do with the Barracuda Mk I, of which, in fact, only thirty examples were built, for, by the time I came into contact with this angular, ugly Fairey product, the prototype of the rather more powerful Mk II was already flying and this was to be the first service version. The Barracuda II differed from its predecessor primarily in having a Merlin 32, affording 1,640hp at 3,000rpm and driving a four-bladed Rotol propeller. The boost gauge now registered +18 pounds on take-off rather than the +12 of the earlier model, and the result was a respectable improvement in getting airborne.

I had not entirely parted company with the sadly underpowered Barracuda Mk I, however, for, on 12 June 1943 I was to find myself in one low over Dunino airfield, a little grass satellite just south of St Andrews of golf fame, the purpose of the flight being radio altimeter trials. The readouts from the altimeter were being checked against a system which involved trailing an aerial to which was attached a substantial lead weight, and as the runs got progressively lower the aerial was wound in by the observer. The final stages of the trial called for slow runs so low that it had been decided to lower the flaps and undercarriage so that ground contact would warn me to climb higher without, it was hoped, damaging the aircraft. A slight power loss caused by boost capsule trouble ensured that ground contact was indeed made. I hurriedly opened up to full power, but, to my astonishment, Barracuda and ground remained in contact! By this time, we had reached and passed the airfield boundary, proving the point in no uncertain terms by passing through some telephone wires and a small tree, bouncing on a hillock and settling gracefully into a ploughed field, where a combination of Scottish stone dyke

Below: Whilst serving at the Royal Aircraft Establishment at Farnborough, Captain Brown explored the capabilities of Barracuda in many and various ways, even taking aloft one aircraft equipped with an airborne lifeboat. The arrangement proved practicable, but was not widely employed.

Above: Perhaps the most bizarre configuration enjoyed by the Barracuda was that by P9795/G, which amongst its duties tested a pair of slab-sided underwing containers for transporting personnel behind enemy lines.

and a series of anti-invasion glider stakes finally halted our progress but removed the Barracuda's mighty undercarriage. Subsequent investigation revealed that the trailing aerial had contacted the ground and that the combined co-efficient of friction of the undercarriage wheels and trailing aerial had been just enough to tip us over the backside of the depleted power curve.

That was to be my last experience with the initial model of the Barracuda. I had first flown its production successor, the Mk II, during the previous April, and, unfortunately for my assessment of this more powerful version, I had flown the Grumman Avenger some two weeks previously and had been so favourably impressed that it had left me rather appalled by the equivalent state of the art in the United Kingdom. Of course, the TSR boys were, by this time, working up on the Barracuda II, 827 Squadron, at RNAS Stretton in Cheshire, having received its aircraft at the beginning of the year, and the first reports had begun to reach us of aircraft diving into the sea, sometimes inverted, while simulating torpedo attacks. As the frequency of such accidents increased, it became progressively more difficult simply to attribute such disasters to the unfamiliarity of ex-biplane crews with monoplane performance, as was the initial tendency.

Meanwhile, I had moved on to the Royal Aircraft Establishment at Farnborough, where I found myself up to the neck in investigating these Barracuda losses, which, by now, totalled five. I was well aware that the torpedo attack technique was to dive to low altitude using the dive flaps, level out, launch the torpedo, retract the flaps and make a rapid and evasive breakaway to one side. This latter phase of the manoeuvre seemed the obvious area for suspicion, and I recollected the rudder overbalance that I had sensed during my first flight in a Barracuda. I therefore performed a series of sideslips at height and at various speeds, deliberately stalling the rudder. When the rudder overbalanced, the nose dropped quite sharply. I also checked the change of trim when the dive brakes were retracted at the bottom of a high-speed dive, and this was markedly nose down.

The next stage was to try out the combination manœuvre. I alerted the flight observer to switch on the cameras recording the instruments giving airspeed, altitude and elevator, rudder and aileron angles, and then put the aircraft into a dive to 210 knots with the flaps in the dive position and with the elevator trimmed to hold it steady. I then simulated levelling out at sea level, and when the speed had dropped below 190 knots—the restriction speed for retracting the dive flaps—I raised the flaps to cruise position and kicked on rudder as I pulled away to starboard. In a flash the aircraft was in an inverted dive! Fortunately, I had plenty of altitude in which to sort out the recovery, but I shuddered at the thought of what the inevitable consequences would have been had I actually performed the test at sea level.

Luckily, the results of this and a number of similar flights were analysed and an appropriate warning issued to all TSR aircrew, the epidemic of crashes ending immediately, but I cannot leave this accident investigation without paying tribute to one of the flight observers involved in these tests, Mrs Gwen Alston. Mrs Alston was a truly remarkable 'lady boffin', who, despite having lost her scientist husband in a fatal crash while on similar duty, never flinched at any risky flight and in all circumstances displayed the essence of courage. She had been my observer on the first flight in which we ascertained the true cause of the Barracuda crashes.

Over the next two years, I was to fly the Barracuda spasmodically in its various versions up to the final Mk V, but throughout it was to remain for me a singularly uninspiring aircraft.

Notes to Ferry Pilots *Courtesy Commander David Hobbs* MBE

Barracuda D. A. II [*sic*] Aircraft

Preliminary Check by Pilot
See that hand rails are up, all back cockpit and side windows closed. A.S.I. cover removed. Superficial glance round the aircraft to make sure that all panels are secure.

Starting Up
    Propeller in fine pitch.
    Electric circuit on.
    Priming cock on.
    Unscrew priming pump.
    Give 4/5 strokes if engine is hot.
      " 7/8 " " " " cold.
    Leave pump drawn back.
    Engine cartridge in breech.
    Switch starter on.
    Main ignition on.
    Open throttles 1".
    Press on start button. (Keep button pressed until engine is properly turning over.)

The engine should start at once. If difficulties are experienced, and while propeller is still revolving, open throttle up to 1½" and when engine is running screw back priming pump, shut priming cock, switch off starter, shut radiator, and let engine warm up at about 1,000 r.p.m.

Running Up and Test
Whilst engine is warming, try hydraulics by exercising flaps down and up, at the same time watch brake pressure gauge which should indicate up to 2,500 lbs. per sq. inch, and cut down to approximately 2,000 lbs. When coolant gauge shows about 60/70° and oil 30° open radiator. Open throttle to +4 boost, and 2,500 revs., test ignition, maximum permissible rev, drop should not exceed 100 r.p.m. Test pitch by reducing revolutions down to 2,000. Throttle back, pull over-ride and test for power by slowly opening throttle to maximum. Revolutions should reach 3,000 r.p.m. boost +18, on no account should the engine be kept at that rate for more than five to ten seconds. While testing for power, it is recommended that two men ride on the end of the fuselage.

Taxying
Barracudas are rather blind forward, care must therefore be taken while taxying. Throttle must be used smoothly. Brakes are powerful and on no account must be kept on for more than a few seconds at a time, otherwise one incurs a risk of burning the tyres.

Take Off
When about to take off, adjust seat height, length of rudder, in other words one has to make oneself comfortable. Give flaps about 15° positive inclination, returning lever to neutral position. Make sure propeller is in fine pitch, tighten throttle, ascertain elevator and rudder trim are at zero. Pull out over-ride, open throttle gently, at the same time check swing to the left by applying sufficient rudder to the right immediately from the start, push stick fully forward to bring tail up in the minimum of time. The aircraft gathering speed will have a tendency to lift too early which will only result in a flop back to the ground, bouncing up again "Kangaroo" fashion. The aircraft must therefore be kept on the ground by use of the stick and not let off prematurely.

Any experienced pilot should feel when the aircraft is ready to fly. Let the aircraft climb slowly in a straight line. When positively sure that the aircraft is flying, retract undercarriage. As soon as the lever is in the 'UP' position two red lights will appear and the green light disappear. As soon as the wheels are locked in the 'UP' position the RED lights will also disappear and no light will be shown. As soon as the undercarriage is locked, throttle back gently to +8 boost and reduce revs. to 2,700 r.p.m. As soon as a speed of about 120 knots and a height of about 300 feet is [*sic*] reached put flaps in normal position, trim rudder and elevator. For normal flights, the best climbing speed is 110/115 knots +7 boost, 2,700 to 2,750 revs.

The most economical and comfortable speed is +2 to +4 boost, 2,000 to 2,400 r.p.m. The aircraft speed should be 120–130 knots. Maximum safe endurance is 4½ to 5 hours.

Point to Watch during Flight
Coolant should be kept between 90° and 100°. This is obtained by adequate opening and shutting the radiator. Maximum permissible 135[°] for five minutes, minimum advisable 85°. Oil temperature normal 60/80°, maximum permissible 100° for five minutes, oil pressure normal

60/90 lbs., minimum permissible 45 lbs. for five minutes. If fuel tank pressure drops a red light will appear, if so land as soon as possible. Brake pressure gauge should keep steady between 2,000 to 2,500 lbs. If it drops below 1,000 lbs. or exceeds 3,000 lbs, put undercarriage down and land as soon as possible.

Fuel

The total of fuel carried in the aircraft is 230 gallons, distributed as follows:-

    1 Main tank containing 90 gallons in each wing.
    1 small tank containing 25 gallons in each wing.

The fuel gauges are situated on the pilot dashboard, and are automatic but do not register more than 75 gallons for each wing. When the level of the tanks of one of the wings reaches 70 gallons or less, the gauge shows the quantity left in that wing. As both tanks do not flow at the same time, the other gauge will not at first show any consumption but should start to do so when the other tank is down to 45 gallons. If the level is reached by one of the gauges and nothing happens to the other gauge, the pilot is advised to wait until the decreasing gauge shows 30 gallons, and if still nothing happens to the other gauge it is advisable to land at the first opportunity as the probability is that the petrol is not flowing from the other tank.

General Flying

The aircraft properly trimmed is steady. Turns are mainly made on the stick. Very little rudder is needed for gentle turns, top rudder is necessary in steeper turns. Negative flaps are only used in steep diving from high altitudes (this does not apply to our kind of work).

It is advisable for Ferry Pilots not to do turns or violent manœuvres at speed lower than 120 knots or exceeding 200 knots.

Landing

When about to land, reduce speed to about 120 knots, boost to zero, engage propeller into fully fine pitch, pull out over-ride, open throttle again to maintain speed of 120 knots. Bring undercarriage down by putting lever in the down position. Two red lights will show and will be replaced by two green lights as soon as the undercarriage is locked in the down position. The locking down of the wheels is also felt by the pilot as they audibly click down, furthermore, part of the undercarriage when down can be seen by the pilot. If not properly locked down a hooter will blow and a red light flickers as soon as the throttle is three quarters closed. When all these operations are completed, and when the last turn has been made at a speed of 120 knots and the aircraft is in a straight landing line, reduce speed to 90 knots and trim elevator accordingly. When about to land bring flap down by pushing lever right down in fully positive position. These flaps are very effective and seem to stop the aircraft in mid air. Some throttle or a steep nose down attitude will therefore be necessary to keep the speed of 85 to 90 knots required. The rest of the landing is easy. The run is short and no difficulty should be experienced.

Mis-landing

If for some reason the pilot decides not to land at the last moment, open throttle fully, raise undercarriage immediately, and when 300 to 400 ft. from the ground raise flaps slowly by bringing lever control to the 'UP' position and 'NEUTRAL' position. (This operation should only be carried out at speeds over 120 knots.)

Below: A Barracuda Mk II of 798 Squadron. The aircraft is in immaculate finish and uncoded, suggesting that the photograph may well have been taken during its initial delivery flight to the unit at Lee-on-Solent. The new exhaust system is fitted, but the channel for the old one is not plated over.

Above: The first Blackburn-built Barracuda, BV660, emerges from the Brough assembly line, 24 September 1942. Six hundred and thirty-four more would follow. This one has a three-bladed propeller, so is doubtless fitted with the Merlin 30 engine rather than the 32.

Difficulties in Bringing Undercarriage Down
If for some reason the undercarriage does not come down properly, check:- Brake pressure gauge, if normal, try undercarriage controls in the 'UP' and 'DOWN' position again, two or three times—it will probably work. If brake pressure gauge is low, 500 lbs. or nothing, keep undercarriage control in the 'Down' position, and pump wheels down (about 100 pumps will be necessary). If no result is obtained, use emergency landing gear as described in the aircraft.

After Landing
Bring flaps up in normal position, push over-ride in.

To Stop Motor
Propeller in fully fine pitch, let motor idle for one minute, pull cut-out, magneto switch 'off', electric circuit, petrol 'off', radiator shut.

Compass
A D.R. [direct reading] Compass is fitted in the tail of the aircraft and a repeater on the pilot's dashboard. To use it:- switch on, switch to "Setting" for about two to three minutes then switch to normal. Bring the pointer for the given degree of course intended to fly and turn the nose of the aircraft until this pointer appears in the middle of the two white lines painted on the top of the compass repeater. On no account switch compass off until this aircraft is definitely parked.

Special Points to Note on Barracuda II—Daily Inspection
Engine
(1) The radiators must be vented with the engine COLD and all air allowed to come out before the coolant level in the Header tank is checked. The venting taps are situated one of top of each radiator—these are to be wire locked. This must be done whenever the engine is allowed to cool.
(2) The drain collector tank must be emptied. The drain tap will be found protruding through the centre of the under-cowling immediately in front of the Fireproof bulkhead. CORRECT OIL D.T.D. [Directorate of

Below: The last Barracuda to be built by Blackburn Aircraft, MX907, is handed over to the Air Transport Auxiliary pilot who will ferry the aircraft to its designated Royal Navy holding unit, 22 June 1945. Its torpedo crutches and bomb racks are *in situ*.

Technical Development] 4572 B and no other. PETROL 100 octane (green) only. COOLANT 33c/559 B – Colour:- Chocolate brown or lemon.

Airframe
(1) Check initial air pressure in brake accumulator (situated on starboard side of fuselage immediately behind the fireproof bulkhead). This should be 300 lbs. per sq. inch, with the Pilots Hydraulic Brake Pressure Gauge in the port bottom side of the pilot's cockpit reading ZERO. The minimum brake pressure allowable is 200 lbs. per sq. inch.
(2) Check the initial air pressure in the main accumulator situated on the port side of the fuselage, the gauge showing this pressure will be seen from the Observer's Port Bay window. With all Hydraulic Pressure released by operation of the Flap Selector Lever, the air pressure should be 1500 lbs. per sq. inch and not less than 1200 lbs. per sq. inch.
(3) Check the level of fluid in the hydraulic header tank (port side of cockpit hooding) with all pressure released. Use only Lockheed Blue to specification D.T.D. 391.
(4) See that the Trailing Edge Selector Lever on the Port Stub Plane of inside the Port Observer's Bay Window is moved to 'spread' position.
(5) The rain extension on the oleo legs should be 3" to 4". Use only anti-freeze oil D.T.D 443 in oleo. Main oleo air pressure should be 250 lbs. per sq. inch.
(6) The tail oleo should protrude from the fuselage so that the frictional vibration damper on the oleo cylinder is partly visible. Use only anti-freeze oil of D.T.D 443 in the leg. Air pressure to be 400 lbs. per sq. inch.

Electrical
(1) Check for correct reading petrol contents, gauges, air temperature and flap indicators controlled by undercarriage switch all situated on pilot's instrument panel.
(2) Check undercarriage indicator lights (Green for Down lock position).
(3) Switch on D.R. Compass. (Switch situated on Pilot's instrument panel). Observe the scale of the master compass through the small panel or window on the port side just aft of dinghy and set the pilot's repeater (situated on instrument panel) the same plus 'A' error marked on master compass.
Note. D.R. will not read correctly if aircraft accumulators fall below 22 volts.

Locking Struts
These are stored in a zip bag in the Port rear part of the pilot cockpit.

Opposite page: Barracuda DT856 (as chalked on one of the propeller blades) under maintenance at the Reserve Aircraft Pool in Gibraltar, revealing the Merlin's two large engine coolant radiators with the oil cooler radiator between. Notice the temporary canvas accommodation in the background.

Above: MD717 is test-flown by the manufacturers, Blackburn, prior to its delivery to the Navy. As is the custom, the bare essentials in terms of markings—national insignia, serial number and service destination—are worn; the application of code letters was the preserve of the receiving unit.

SPECIFICATIONS
FAIREY BARRACUDA Mks I–V

Manufacturer:	The Fairey Aviation Company Ltd, Hayes, Middlesex. Production at Heaton Chapel, by Blackburn Aircraft Ltd at Brough, by Boulton Paul Aircraft Ltd at Wolverhampton and by Westland Aircraft Ltd at Yeovil.
Chief Designer:	Marcelle Lobelle.
Powerplant:	One Rolls-Royce Merlin 30 (Mks II, III Merlin 32, Mk V Griffon 37) V12 liquid-cooled inline engine developing 1,260hp (Mks II, III 1,640hp, Mk V 2,020hp).
Dimensions:	Length overall 39ft 9in (12.12m); wing span (Mks I–III) 49ft 2in (14.99m), (Mk V) 53ft 0½in (16.17m) spread, 19ft 6in (5.94) folded; height (Mks I–III, early Mk V) 15ft 1½in (4.61m), (later Mk V) 17ft 3in (5.26m) tail down; wing area (gross) (Mks I–III) 405.0 sq ft (37.63m^2), Mk V 435 sq ft (40.41m^2).
Weights:	8,700lb (3,950kg), (Mk II) 9,350lb (4,240kg), (Mk III) 9,410lb (4,270kg), (Mk V) 11,430lb (5,185kg) empty; 11,900lb (5,400kg), (Mk II) 13,200lb (5,985kg), (Mk III) 13,300lb (6,030kg), (Mk V) 15,250lb (6,915kg) normal loaded.
Armament:	(Mks I–III) One flexibly mounted Vickers 0.303in machine gun ('K' gun) with 200rds/barrel in observer's cockpit (generally removed) and one pair flexibly mounted Vickers 0.303in machine guns ('K' guns) with 500rds/barrel in TAG's cockpit, (Mk V) one fixed, forward-firing 0.50in Browning machine gun with 200rds, plus (all marks) one 18in (45.7cm), 1,610lb (730kg) torpedo or 1,600lb (725kg) bomb or 1,500lb (680kg) sea mine beneath fuselage or maximum external underwing load (bombs, sea mines or depth charges) of 2,000lb (907kg).
Performance:	Maximum speed 204kts (235mph, 380kph) at 11,000ft (3,350m), (Mk II) 198kts (228mph, 366kph) at 1,750ft (535m), (Mk III) 208kts (239mph, 395kph) at 1,750ft, (Mk V) 220kts (253mph, 407kph) at 10,000ft (3,050m); economical cruising speed 120kts (138mph, 222kph) at 6,000ft (1,830m), (Mk II) 150kts (172mph, 277kph) at 5,000ft (1,525m), (Mk III) 148kts (170mph, 274kph) at 5,000ft; service ceiling 18,400ft (5,600m), (Mk II) 16,600ft (5,050m), (Mk III) 20,000ft (6,100m), (Mk V) 24,000ft 7,315m); range 455nm (525 miles, 845km), (Mk III) 595nm (685 miles, 1,100km), (Mk V) 520nm (600 miles, 965km).
Number built:	(Excl. prototype, pre-production and converted aircraft) 2,600 (30 Mk Is, 1,688 Mk IIs, 852 Mk IIIs, 30 Mk Vs). Totals for the Mks II and III are unconfirmed: many aircraft identified as Mk IIIs in production lists (e.g., with serials in the PM- and PN- ranges) were actually completed as Mk IIs and entered service as such. The reason for the discrepancies may concern equipment shortages.

BARRACUDA

Nobody to Say You Nae *Third Officer Joy Lofthouse ATA*

I was only sixteen when war broke out, working for Lloyd's Bank but wondering whether I could join the forces when I was old enough. I had no family connection with flying, but the countryside around my home had been changing rapidly as more and more airfields—Kemble, Aston Down, Little Rissington, etc.—were constructed, most of them to provide training facilities. In the summer of 1943 I saw a newspaper article remarking on the fact that the Air Training Auxiliary were running out of qualified pilots and were now training *ab initio*. That was for me!

I was trained from scratch—I couldn't even drive a car at the time. The ATA was a civilian organisation. We did not swear allegiance to the Crown nor did we hold the King's Commission. We were paid by the Ministry of Aircraft Production. We wore uniform, and because our founder happened to be a director of BOAC this was very like that of civilian airline staff—navy blue with gold 'wings', and with badges of rank worn on the shoulder. We had our own training school at Thame, near Oxford.

I was accepted into the Service in August 1943 but my bank manager would not release me at first and I was not able to begin flying until December that year (much to my chagrin: my older sister was able to start before me, in September!). It was therefore winter before I was able to begin, which meant that bad weather frequently interrupted the schedules. Perhaps surprisingly, we trained on Magisters: Tiger Moths were employed only in order to enable us to practise recovering from spins (the Miles aircraft being not particularly adept in this respect). Once the instructor felt that you were up to the job, you were checked out by the CO, went solo and then flew cross-countries to get used to navigation. You were then sent to a pool to do some taxi work flying Fairchild Arguses and to gain experience flying other types of training aircraft, and then it was back to Thame to convert to Harvards. More general experience flying, and cross-countries, followed, until the day came—in my case, some five months after I had joined the ATA—when you were directed to a corner of the airfield where an early-mark Spitfire was waiting. The Big Day! Once you had successfully flown the Spitfire—a daunting task at first, considering that you were now, for the first time, alone in a high-performance fighter—you were qualified on Class 1 and Class 2 aircraft, that is, trainers and single-engined fighters.

My permanent pool was now at Hamble, from where, to my delight, a lot of Spitfires were being collected from the Supermarine factory at Eastleigh and flown to MUs. My first encounter with the Barracuda came in early 1945, when I was at Thame. I remember the flight very well because I was in company with another Barracuda and the weather clamped in over the Cotswolds. My companion flew in very close to me and started to point downwards vigorously, and we found a gap in the clouds and landed at Moreton-in-Marsh, where we were stranded for a couple of days.

Below: An Air Transport Auxiliary pilot—believed to be the American John Yingst—prepares to leave Ringway in Barracuda II LS855 some time in 1944. Ringway was home to ATA Ferry Pool 14. Two Ansons are also seen in the photograph, one to the right and the second in the distance; the twin on the left is an Airspeed Oxford.

Above ATA personnel pose in front of a Blackburn-built Barracuda at Sherburn-in-Elmet. Joy Lofthouse is in the centre of the group.

Having read and digested the Ferry Pilot's Notes of course (see pages 40–44), and having made a few flights, I found the Barracuda easy to fly, although the landing had been a little surprising as the aircraft was much higher from the ground on touch-down than I had been used to. Limitations were 1,500 yards (take-off) and 800 feet (cloud cover). In really clear, sunny weather, we could indulge ourselves by flying a little higher than normal. There was always plenty of time, too: my logbook tells me that practically all my Barracuda flights lasted over an hour, because of the aircraft's leisurely progress compared to that of, say, a Spitfire.

I flew a few more Barracudas from Hamble, but when this facility closed in May 1945 I moved to Sherburn-in-Elmet, from where Blackburn-built Barracudas from nearby Brough were delivered to Royal Navy acceptance units. RNAS Crail and, in particular, RNAS Dunino, were frequent destinations for me. This was a busy time, because we were taking naval aircraft to the Scottish bases, from where they would be embarked on aircraft carriers destined for the war in the Far East. I was en route to Crail when I experienced my only real spot of difficulty in a Barracuda. It has to be remembered that there was no communications equipment on board these aircraft, and navigation had to be carried out by the ATA pilot (who was on his or her own) with nothing more than a map and a compass. For this reason, we always flew within sight of the ground; and, for reasons of economy, we always flew straight and level, and at optimal cruising speed, so as to minimise fuel consumption. On this particular flight, while crossing the Firth of Forth I encountered the well-known Scottish haar. I was particularly relieved to be flying a Barracuda: as the saying went at the time, this was an aircraft that, if you put the wheels and the flaps down, would fly backwards! There was therefore, to my relief, time enough to think. I climbed, did a 180-degree turn, and set course for RAF Acklington on the Northumberland coast, where I landed safely. I completed the flight to Crail once the weather had improved.

Because there was no radio equipment for ferry flights, landings were made according to our own judgement and we joined the circuit when all appeared to be clear and we received a 'green'. This could be a bit of a problem if we happened to arrive at a particularly busy time. Upon landing, the procedure was to taxi to the tower, whereupon we would be directed that part of the airfield where the aircraft was required. Towards the end of the war we received strict instructions regarding strange looking aircraft with a very short endurance, and were told that these had to be given absolute priority. The aircraft were, of course, Meteors.

As for overnight accommodation, at service airfields we were always put up in the Mess (and the WAAF's Mess—the 'Waafery'—was always the coldest Nissan hut on the station, so if this kind of stopover was anticipated we came prepared with hot water bottles!). Where there were civilian ATA establishments, as at Hamble, Thame and Sherburn, we had private billeting.

I flew eighteen different types altogether, including Oxfords, Ansons, Hellcats and, on a couple of occasions, a Dauntless. The wonderful thing about ferry flying was that, once you were in the air, nobody could 'say you nae'—you were completely your own master or mistress. There was no 'technical' training involved, no blind-flying, no bad-weather flying and no night-flying. It was simply wonderful!

LEARNING TO FIGHT

Lieutenant-Commander Robert McCandless DSC

WE were all very pleased to get away from RAF Errol and arrive at RN Air Station Crail (HMS *Jackdaw*). At last we were into a proper Fleet Air Arm environment where the accommodation was warm and comfortable and of course, there were lots of attractive Wrens around with whom we were allowed to fraternise at the weekly Station Dance. All very enjoyable!

Our instructors were nearly all Lieutenants (A) RNVR and the CO of the Squadron (785) was Lieutenant-Commander Thorpe RN (he did look young—even to us sprogs). Most of them had done their operational flying in Swordfish with a fairly short spell on Barracudas which had occurred during the period of development described earlier. The result was that they were not fully confident about the aircraft, and when they were briefing us on the cockpit and on flying the machine there were a lot of dire warnings. In the event we had no fatal accidents on our course and all went according to plan.

To begin with, we flew around the local area and got used to handling the aircraft. I found it comfortable and easy to handle. Take-off was very straightforward, without any swing or torque effect, and right from the earliest take-offs we were encouraged to jink to starboard immediately after getting airborne with the intention of clearing the runway of slipstream so that aircraft taking off close behind would have less turbulence just at the point where they were becoming airborne. This was standard practice at the time with short-interval take-offs (less than 30 seconds) from airfield or carrier.

After about four hours of familiarisation flying we started to get used to carrying a load. This was a dummy torpedo made of concrete with dimensions similar to the operational torpedo which we could carry in anger, should the occasion arise.

The next step was to practise and get used to the feel of low flying over the sea: we were going to be doing this regularly, so we were encouraged to dive

Below: Thirty-six Barracuda IIs of 711, 785 and 786 Squadrons (RNAS Crail) in the spring of 1945. This was usually the final exercise at the end of the torpedo course. It was referred to as a 'balbo' and simulated a co-ordinated 'attack' on one target at sea. It made all the students wonder about mid-air collisions, but, in the event, there never were any.

Above: Six Barracuda IIs from 829 Squadron, on a training flight from RNAS Lee-on-Solent in October or November 1943. The nearest trio each carry an underbelly 1,610-pound (18-inch) torpedo equipped with a stabilising 'air tail', the latter assisting a smooth entry into the water at the correct angle. The engine exhausts on these aircraft have evidently been modified post-production: notice the plating-over of the original angled troughs.

quite steeply down to the water and try to judge our height, aiming to be at 100 feet.

Then it was a matter of starting to practise making individual torpedo attacks on a ship at sea. These attacks were assessed by Wren Range Assessors from the F.46 camera, which took a timed photograph at the instant of pressing the release button, and with knowledge of the ship's course and speed and any avoiding action at that time, plus the recorded settings from the torpedo control sight, they were able to give fairly accurate assessments of the attack. For logbook entries, these camera attacks were designated ALT.*

As we became more competent and confident we moved on to carrying out attacks as a group, and gradually the formations got larger. The smallest group was usually six aircraft flying in three pairs line astern and the larger groups were in multiples giving twelve or eighteen; the largest group in which I took part comprised 36 aircraft. When we flew as a formation to carry out a combined torpedo attack, it was standard practice to synchronise the clocks in the cameras so that the assessors could calculate the precise intervals between the individual torpedo drops and know what action the target was taking at that time, and so calculate if each aircraft had scored a hit or miss. There were occasions when pilots inadvertently activated the arming switch as well as the camera switch and dummy torpedoes were dropped from a couple of thousand feet over land. There were many apocryphal stories about where they landed, such as vertically in the graveyard in Crail village, or in the back yard of the police house, but I never heard of any damage caused by this careless error. Rear-Admiral I. G. W. Robertson CB DSC recalls that 'in 1944, during a dummy torpedo dropping exercise from RNAS Crail, one of the students, Sub-Lieutenant Jordan, was taking off with his concrete torpedo and was hugely surprised to find that

---

* See footnote on page 12.

BARRACUDA

it had released without any action on his part and gone into the wardroom! Luckily, lunch had finished and the room was empty.'

Altogether at Crail, we carried out about eighty practice torpedo attacks of which many were individual, four were ADT and five were ART. During this time we had a variety of vessels acting as targets, the largest of which was probably HMS *Dauntless*. We tried to use any of the naval vessels entering or leaving the Forth on their way to and from Rosyth.

The drill we were taught and practised regularly was to aim to fly across the bow of the target a mile or so ahead with the aircraft in three pairs, long line astern (about 500 yards between pairs), to give sufficient separation to divide the attention of the enemy's anti-aircraft gunners. Then all six aircraft entered a steep dive together, still heading across the target's line of advance. In the dive we selected 'dive brakes' and trimmed the elevator 2½ turns nose-down. During this straight dive down, we had to assess the ship's speed and set it on the control. Then we had to estimate our bearing from the ship. The first pair might be 25 degrees on the starboard bow, the second pair dead ahead on 0 degrees and the third pair 30 degrees on the port bow. Each pilot would turn his torpedo control switch to the appropriate figure for his own aircraft, assuming that 0 degrees represented the ship's heading on a steady course.

When a ship is moving at speed, the wake is clearly defined. When the rudder is moved hard over to one side to alter course quickly, it causes a 'blip' on the side of the wake and this shows that the ship is trying to take evasive action by changing direction in a hurry. This blip is fairly noticeable in relatively calm seas, but it does tend to get lost in rough weather. If the Barracuda pilot noticed the blip or saw the change of direction in the wake it was clear that the ship was trying to avoid the torpedoes and he could set the 'avoiding switch' accordingly during the dive.

With the six aircraft on the different bearings, if the target were to show a blip on the port side of the wake, the first pair would set the switch to 'Avoiding away'. The second pair would be in a dilemma and would probably not use the switch at all and just aim off on the port side of the ship, and the third pair

With the Taranto success and the *Bismarck* episode still fresh in the memory, trainee Barracuda aircrews devoted a good deal of their time to torpedo delivery, certainly in 1943-44 when the aircraft was being taken into service in considerable numbers. In the event, however, Barracudas were employed as torpedo bombers only very rarely, dive bombing becoming preferred as the most efficacious method of attacking enemy shipping. Here a torpedo-armed P9667—an early-production aircraft and, curiously, lacking the Barracuda's characteristic underwing leeboards—enters a shallow descent. The photograph is interesting also in that it is one of the few that clearly illustrates the little-used—and quickly abandoned—Barracuda observer's machine gun: it is seen angled towards the roof of his cockpit canopy in the stowed position.

would set 'Avoiding towards'. All of these settings would be passed directly into the torpedo and its own steering gyro would, with luck, lead the torpedo in the right direction to hit the moving target. Throughout the dive, the pilot was keeping a close eye on the altitude, so, bearing in mind that the dive lasted about fifteen seconds, he was fully occupied.

When the aircraft was approaching the bottom of the dive, the pilot began his pull-out, imposing fairly hefty 'g' (centrifugal) forces and at the same time turning in towards the target. The intention was to slow down to about 120 knots at 100 feet, when the Youngman flaps were returned to neutral and the elevator trim immediately trimmed back (nose up) two and a half turns.

To try to ensure a clean entry into the water for the torpedo, the latter had a very flimsy aerofoil fitted to its tail to prevent it rolling and to encourage it to make contact with the water slightly nose down. The aerofoil broke off as the torpedo entered the water. The target range should have been about 1,000 yards or less and if there were waves of any significant size the intention would be to drop the torpedo so that it entered the face of an approaching wave. The pilot was then free to make his escape as best he could, everyone turning aft of the target to avoid mid-air collisions.

Setting the torpedo control depended on the pilot and/or observer knowing important facts about the target, and all aircrew were required to study ship recognition a well as aircraft recognition. We had to be able to identify the ship, or at least the class of ship, from any angle, low level or high level, or through brief breaks in the clouds or in poor visibility, and therefore know the top speed and the main and secondary armament. To judge the speed, the turbulence of the wake and the size of the bow wave were taken into account.

The assessed results of every practice attack were recorded as a graph on a chart which was designed in such a way that each element of the attack could be joined on to previous records. Thus we had a continuous graph covering the whole course. The information was recorded according to the type of attack (ALT, ADT or ART); the target (ship's name and speed at the time); ship's action (steady course, or avoiding port or starboard); aircraft's position (relative to the ship, angle off the bow); time (at which time during the ship's actions the torpedo would have been dropped, and whether this was before or after the leader's drop); hit or miss (the target was assumed to be 400 feet long and a direct hit was amidships, although a hit was still registered if the assessed strike was plus or minus 200 feet of the midpoint); and calculation error (which assessed the pilot's errors either in not aiming directly at the target or in putting the wrong settings on the torpedo control switch). In addition, the sighting error (aim), range in yards, height of the aircraft in feet and attitude of the aircraft (nose up or down and wings level) were recorded as a graph which was continued throughout the course whichever type of attack, individually or in groups. From these graphs and recorded details the instructors were able to help the students to correct errors which were being repeated.

The five ART attacks in formation were the culmination of our course at Crail. We moved *en masse* from there to the RNAS East Haven (HMS *Peewit*) for our final weapon training course, leaving behind any girlfriends as sailors tend to do.

We joined 769 Squadron at East Haven in the middle of April and stayed for four weeks. During this period we had practice sessions of dive bombing, depth-charge dropping, ADDLs (Aerodrome Dummy Deck Landings), carrier procedures for take-off and landing (individually and in formation, by day and by night), fighter evasion and cross-country navigation exercises. Three sorties a day was standard procedure, four trips not uncommon, and one day I did five, including two 45-minute sorties at night. The training was quite intensive.

The practice dive bombing was carried out individually. The aircraft was loaded with eight practice bombs as already described. When we took off we would climb to something above 10,000 feet and contact the range assessors by radio. When they were ready for us, they would give permission to start the exercise. We always gave our call-sign as we entered the dive so that their recording of the bomb burst was applied to the right pilot.

It was intended that the dive should be at 70 degrees and, for each attack, so that the range assessors could record the angle of dive, we always started the dive from the same position relative to the target, This meant that we tracked across the assessor's line of sight and she was able to mark the aircraft's position all the way down the dive.

Left: P9667 a few frames further on, now entering the dive proper; notice that the Youngman flaps have been moved to negative incidence for the purpose. On entering the dive, the elevator trim would be wound forward slightly—this effect can just be discerned in the photograph.

Right: Two more views of Barracudas at Crail; in the upper photograph, the pair furthest from the camera are Mk Is, with three-bladed propellers. Once the basics of TBR had been mastered, Barracuda pilots moved north to RNAS East Haven, across the Firth of Tay, where other attack procedures were learnt, together with the all-important skills of carrier deck landing (Aerodrome Dummy Deck Landings, or ADDLs).

Below: A head-on view of a radar-equipped Barracuda, clearly showing the disposition of the underwing stores stations. These could carry 500-pound bombs (maximum two per wing); 250-pound bombs (up to three per wing); depth charges (up to three per wing); mines; or practice bombs (up to twelve per wing). In later years, sonobuoys or smoke floats could be carried.

If the pilot's aim was accurate, but the angle of dive was shallow, the bomb would drop short (and this was a frequent error to begin with); the opposite occurred if the dive was too steep. Bearing in mind that the wings still gave lift while in the dive, it was necessary, with increasing lift as a result of the increasing speed, to keep trimming nose down, otherwise the dive would become increasingly shallow and the target would disappear under the nose of the aircraft. Therefore, the attitude of the aircraft continually altered during the dive until it was practically vertical and the pilot was hanging in his straps (which latter, therefore, had to be really tight before starting the dive—as had the observer's and the TAG's).

From experience, it had been shown that releasing the bomb as close to the target as one dared was likely to give greater accuracy of delivery. This was somewhat off-putting for the *ab initio* trainee: there he was, pointing straight at the ground and with his height rapidly decreasing. Some dropped from too high and thus the bomb would fall short, and some frightened themselves rigid by leaving it almost too late. The point of release and the point of starting the pull-out from the dive tended to coincide, but if the pull-out started a split second before the release the bomb could be thrown quite a long way over. It took a lot of training to get everything right.

In a crosswind, which was very often present, it was necessary to take action to avoid being blown off target. The procedure was quite regular because all that was required was to lower the wing on the side from which the wind was blowing, as if turning into it. The stronger the wind, the more the wing would be lowered. It was always better to try to anticipate this and put the control column over right at the top of the dive, while the airspeed was low, and hold it there all the way down in the dive, incorporating it into the normal aiming.

In an operational attack on a ship, because circumstances might not allow the angle of dive to be absolutely precise, the direction of the dive to the target was always intended to be along the fore-and-aft line of the ship. Unfortunately things did not always work out that way, and the pilot had to use his own experience to adjust his aiming point.

At the bottom of the dive, after dropping one bomb, we pulled out (imposing heavy 'g' forces on the aircraft and on ourselves), aiming to use the speed from the dive to help us climb back quickly to the correct altitude, and this was repeated for all eight bombs, after which we returned to the airfield to change pilots, reload with eight more bombs and refuel if necessary. In this way, even if there was more than one aircraft on the bombing range at the same time, we were all credited with the correct recordings of our own bombing errors.

Although it was during the month of April, it was still quite chilly on the east coast of Scotland, enough to justify wearing fairly warm flying clothing, including the fleece-lined flying boots. These were very loose and slipped up and down as I walked, wearing holes in my socks. My darning was never up to much so, to stop that happening, I put strong parachute elastic round each ankle to stop the boots slipping, and this was quite successful.

When we were first being briefed on torpedo attack at Crail, one of the instructors suggested that it would be prudent if I were to keep the cockpit hood open during the dive, first for better visibility all round and secondly to help with a speedy exit should anything go wrong. I had done this and continued it during dive bombing.

On each dive, I found myself blacking out either partially or fully for a few seconds while pulling out of the dive, and my colleagues admitted that they too were affected by the heavy 'g' as they recovered from each dive. So I accepted this as normal. However, on my fifth sortie, at the bottom of the third dive the port wing came off my aircraft, which went into an immediate and very violent spin. I yelled to the observer to bail out and pulled my harness release clip. I was immediately thrown out of the aircraft by the violence of the spin and my parachute opened just in time to stop me hitting the water. There had been no time to think about it. All my actions were quite automatic from having considered it all previously—when something might go wrong, what I should do about it, and precisely what actions I would have to take. (This is what I have done with every aircraft I have ever flown and, in fact, when I move into a room in a hotel, one of my first actions is to check the quickest route to the nearest fire escape, or in a cruise ship, the quickest route to the

Left: A pair of 500-pound bombs with a some morale-boosting additions on the two inboard stations of the port wing of 831 Squadron Barracuda 'M'.
Right, top: Minelaying was another task assigned to Barracudas: here a 400-pound mine is displayed, with its loading trolley in position.
Right, bottom: Subjected to trials at A&AEE Boscombe Down but not taken into service with Barracudas was the 250-pound 'SCI Container'—a device for laying a smokescreen. One is fitted beneath each wing on this aircraft, P9652, an early Mk I.

designated boat deck!) Because I had entered the water so quickly, I had not had time to release my parachute. Luckily there was enough wind to carry the canopy away so that it did not settle over me, so on releasing the parachute harness it all sank immediately and did not get entangled with my legs. I then inflated my Mae West lifejacket and started to swim for the shore four or five hundred yards away.

There were, however, two things that I noticed right away. First, I wasn't making any progress at all because I still had my flying boots on and they were getting heavier. I couldn't kick them off because of the parachute elastic. Secondly, the land was moving past at quite a smart pace because the tide was going outward with the flow of the river. After some considerable effort and underwater contortions, I finally got the boots off and struck out again for the shore. The Wrens from the nearer of the two marker huts were running along the beach trying to keep up as I was being swept out to the North Sea. As I crawled out of the surf, they were there to help me, and I certainly needed their assistance. I must admit that things are very vague after that until I awoke up in the Station Sick Bay.

55

Next day I was examined by the Medical Officer who pronounced me fit to continue with the course. I was told at the same time that my observer's parachute had caught on the tailplane and that he had gone in with the aircraft. That did depress me: it was my fault that he had died and I did regret it—deeply.

I must admit I felt very embarrassed when I went a day or so later to thank the Wrens for their help and, particularly, to thank the Safety Equipment Wren who had packed my parachute. As a callow youth, I didn't know whether to shake her by the hand or clasp her to my bosom and give her a kiss. To be honest, I don't remember what I did!

At the Captain's Inquiry I reported that I was still trimming back as I pulled out of the dive. It was estimated that I had subjected the aircraft to something greater than 7g—much more than the aircraft was built to withstand. No disciplinary action was taken, and two days after the incident I was back flying again, carrying out the same series of exercises (and without any thought of counselling, thank goodness).

We were also trained to drop depth charges. Generally speaking, when we were on a submarine search, we flew individually at whatever height gave us the best visibility, taking cloud and weather into account, but I do not remember ever flying higher than about 4,000 feet because periscopes or snorkel tubes can be quite difficult to see, particularly in sea states greater than 3 (that is, with white wave caps showing). We always assumed that a submarine's crew would be keeping a good watch for aircraft when any part of the boat was above the surface, and so, if we were lucky enough to see a periscope or snorkel, we always took it for granted that the boat would dive immediately. Thus we needed to make our attack without any delay from whatever altitude we happened to be. The intention was to straddle the submarine with four depth charges and hope that this spread would allow for any poor aim on the pilot's part or any underwater change of course on the part of the submarine. The fact is, it was all too easy to lose sight of the periscope if the sea was at all rough, then one had to make an educated guess as to the precise position to drop. If the submarine was on the surface, he had two choices, either to dive if he had seen the aircraft sufficiently far away to give him time to do so, or stay on the surface and fight it out. Perhaps circumstances in the submarine might force him to stay on the surface in any case. Submarine patrols were always carried out by individual aircraft, so no doubt the submarine captain would feel that it was a fairly evenly balanced fight, because of course, with depth charges or A/S bombs, the aircraft had to fly directly over the target to deliver the weapons. Although the Swordfish on the Atlantic patrols were sometimes armed with rocket projectiles, we never employed them in Barracudas. In fact, I seem to recall that we were not fitted to carry them.

There was no sight fitted in the Barracuda to help, so, once again, aiming was a matter of guesswork—improving with experience. The small number of sorties we flew with practice bombs were merely to give us an idea of how and when to drop. These bombs were timed to represent the first and the last of the four depth charges, and our intention was, again, always to straddle the target. We fairly quickly got the hang of it.

Below: A pair of Barracudas flying from RNAS Ronaldsway in the Isle of Man. They belong to No 1 Operational Training Unit (comprising 710, 713 and 747 NAS), whose aircraft tended to be shared around, and have the well-used finish typical of wartime second-line squadron aircraft. The Barracuda nearest the camera (nicknamed 'Mary'—probably a legacy from earlier service in a front-line squadron) is a Mk II, with the original wing-mounted ASV radar array, its companion is a Mk III, with that mark's characteristic ventral radome.

FRONT-LINE FLYING

Lieutenant-Commander Robert McCandless DSC

AFTER leaving RN Air Station East Haven, I had a brief period on leave during which I received the very formal appointment to join 827 Naval Air Squadron on board HMS *Furious* in Scapa Flow on 6 June 1944.

I travelled by slow train from Stirling to Thurso, where I arrived in the middle of the night with my two kit bags. Somehow I found my way to the harbour, where the Kirkwall ferry was preparing to set off on her daily trip. We left the harbour at about 0500 and I certainly knew when we were in the Pentland Firth even though I was down in the saloon because the weather was so rough. That sturdy little ferry was being tossed around like a cork and quite quickly I began to feel distinctly unwell. Luckily, I hadn't eaten since the previous day. I suppose also I was somewhat apprehensive because it was clear to me that I was being appointed to an active front-line squadron to replace aircrew who had been lost during operations.

At 0600 the ferry skipper switched on the public address system to give us the early morning news: 'This is the BBC News, and this is Alvar Liddell reading it. Our forces have landed in Normandy.' Immediately all thoughts of an upset tum left my mind, and I arrived in Kirkwall fully awake, quite excited, and wondering what it might mean for me.

I found my way to the jetty where the libertymen were brought ashore from the ships in Scapa Flow and waited for a boat from HMS *Furious* to arrive and take me and my two kitbags back on board. The boat's crew must have looked at me, resplendent in my new uniform with its bright brass buttons and new gold cap badge, and thought to themselves, 'They certainly catch them young nowadays. Poor b——!' My arrival at the ship and the tussle with my kitbags confirmed to all and sundry that here was a new boy. I saluted at the top of the ladder and awaited the arrival of someone who might know where I was to go.

After a while, a little man in working rig arrived on the quarterdeck and introduced himself as 'Steward Brookfield, Sir. I am your steward in the Squadron,' and he led me off into the bowels of the ship to my sleeping quarters. En route he pointed out the wardroom and anteroom so that I would be able to begin to find my way around. I found that I was to sleep in a sort of dormitory, and this was laid out in a very confusing way, with two-tier bunks and lockers packed in as tightly as possible while still allowing restricted movement amongst them. But what hit me—almost literally—was the stench. There must have been about twenty or more bunks, and I quickly discovered that the ventilation was very poor.

Below: A wartime photograph of HMS *Furious*; the presence of 20mm Oerlikon AA guns around the perimeter of the flight deck indicates 1942 or later. The substantial cylindrical beacon (mounted atop the ship's low island superstructure) was a homing device to aid returning pilots. The disruptive camouflage was intended to help break up the ship's outline and so hamper any U-boat commander who might approach within firing range. *Furious* had performed with distinction in air operations as far back as World War I, when she had launched Camel biplanes for an attack against German Zeppelin sheds in July 1918. Earlier, she had been a hybrid cruiser-aircraft carrier and, when originally designed, a big-gun (18-inch) 'large light cruiser'.

Above: A brand new Barracuda II shows its undersurfaces. Notice the landing light in the port wing leading edge, the six weapons racks and the many jacking pads (the latter showing as dark 'spots') beneath the wings, and the angled housings for the grab handles near the wing tips. The flare chute, beneath the TAG's cockpit and offset to port, can also be made out. This was a hefty airframe to rely for its power on a single 1,600hp Merlin.

The trouble was that *Furious* had originally been constructed as a cruiser and had then been modified several times as naval flying developed between the 1914-18 war and the 1939-45 war. The particular problem was that the ship was now able to carry and operate so many more aircraft—and therefore so many more men, both maintenance ratings and aircrew—that living space throughout was extraordinarily cramped.

I sorted myself out as best I could in the limited space available and by now, as I was feeling somewhat peckish, I found my way to the anteroom, which was already fairly full. My Commanding Officer was pointed out to me. He was standing with a group of 'two-and-a-halfs', so I went over to introduce myself. He turned and looked at me. He didn't even say hello, merely, 'You can get those bloody patches off right now!' Then he summoned one of the 827 Squadron pilots and told him to introduce me. His name was Drew Michie and he hailed from Dunfermline, which was about twelve miles or so from my home. We became good friends and he led me gently through all the introductions to people and routines. I was accepted readily enough and felt that I was going to enjoy myself in this group.

The next time I saw the CO, he welcomed me to the Squadron and noted that I was wearing sub-lieutenant's uniform. He didn't comment on it, but he obviously did not want a midshipman in his aircrew; perhaps he thought that the observers and TAGs who would have to fly with me might have lacked confidence in such a 'sprog' pilot. He was once again with a group of the more senior officers and he asked me if I was the pilot who had managed to bale out of a Barracuda after pulling the wing off during dive bombing. When I admitted that I was, he asked me how it had happened. However, when I explained that it was my fault, he was obviously not pleased because he was one of the aircrew who had been flying in Barracudas throughout the development period and he and his contemporaries firmly believed that it was the aircraft that was at fault—and here was I, the most inexperienced of pilots, saying that it was due to pilot error. Popular I was not.

BARRACUDA

Drew showed me around the parts of the ship that I needed to know, through the hangars and up on to the flight deck. Here he showed me the differences from other carriers and how different our carrier procedure would be from what we had been taught.

By the time I joined HMS *Furious* in 1944 a small island had been added on the starboard side of the flight deck, but this did not include a funnel; with a flag deck on top, it was used almost entirely for communications equipment. The aerials for this equipment were mounted on three masts fitted on each side of the flight deck which at Flying Stations were lowered hydraulically outboard to a horizontal position.

We went first to the after end of the flight deck. There was no round-down as on all modern carriers: it was quite a cliff-edge because there were two huge smoke discharge grilles fitted as close to the stern as possible; moreover, because of the need to range the maximum number of aircraft for launching, it was necessary that the two aircraft—Barracudas—at the back of the launch actually parked on these grilles. The aircrew sitting in the aircraft waiting for take-off before the ship turned into wind were forced to use the aircraft oxygen system—the only time it was ever used!

About 150 feet of the after end of the flight deck was horizontal, and then there was a slight slope down which was intended to help aircraft to pick up speed at the start of their take-off run. Between the smoke grilles and the slope was the after aircraft lift, cruciform in shape so that aircraft with fixed (non-folding) wings could be raised and lowered. Forward of the slope was a level area about 150 feet long in which the arrester gear wires lay across the deck, then came a ramp upwards which, I understand, was intended to help the aircraft to get airborne. This was certainly successful with the Seafires and Wildcats, but a loaded Barracuda invariably leapt into the air then bounced on its main wheels right on the forward end of the flight deck before roaring off in a jink to starboard.

The forward aircraft lift, the same shape as the after lift, was just forward of the ramp and then we came to the forward round-down, which was semi-circular in plan view. At the starboard end of the semi-circle was a cockpit, the Captain's navigating position, and at the port end was another cockpit, the Flying Control position, with a little horizontal mast to display the 'Affirmative' flag. Both cockpits were of such a depth as to allow men of average height to look along the flight deck to see what was

Opposite page: HMS *Furious* had hangars on two levels, and in 1944 the upper was normally populated with Seafires and the lower was reserved for the Barracudas. Here a Barracuda of 827 Squadron is manhandled on to the lift prior to dispatch up to the flight deck.
Above: *Furious*, again during the war, clearly showing the low island superstructure to starboard, the cruciform lifts forward and aft and the notorious smoke discharge grilles aft, upon which waiting Barracudas might steadily blacken. The quarterdeck features a twin 4-inch gun mounting; light anti-aircraft guns were carried in sponsons along the edges of the flight deck.

going on, but on reflection in the light of later experience, their view must have been very restricted and somewhat distorted. Bearing in mind that these two positions were very exposed, the only shelter they had was a very lightweight wood and Perspex windshield. I presume it was constructed in this way so as to minimise damage to any aircraft which might have had an erratic take-off or, going around again, had missed the wires.

I have not mentioned barriers. There were none—and, of course, this brought about a very significant difference from the landing-on drill we had practised at East Haven: it meant that every aircraft had to be struck down before the next aircraft could land-on. If I remember correctly, the fighters used the upper hangar and the Barracudas the lower hangar. The

Left: A trials Barracuda departs from the water-strewn flight deck of the Royal Navy's armoured fleet carrier *Illustrious*, its propeller tips generating vortices in their wake. Opposite page: Handlers rush to assist the marshalling of Barracuda '5A', which has just landed on board *Furious*. Notice the retractable handling rails beneath the aircraft's outer wing panels—these would have been deployed during the approach—and also the gentle undulation in the carrier's flight deck aft, referred to by the author.

Seafires, which did not fold, were taxied on to the lift and struck down, and the lift came back to flight-deck level quite quickly, which meant that their landing interval was probably just over a minute. That for the Wildcats was not very much longer.

However, the Barracudas were a different kettle of fish because they had to be folded by hand and lowered two decks, and then the lift needed to be returned the two decks to flight-deck level. From catching a wire until the lift returned to flight-deck level took about two and a half minutes, and this meant that when a number of Barracudas were landing-on, each pilot after the first had a huge hole in the flight deck throughout his approach; furthermore, just before touch-down he had his view of the deck obscured by his engine. Twelve aircraft landing-on would consume half an hour. Comparing this with a worked-up carrier such as those operating off Korea, when ten aircraft could be landed-on in less than five minutes, it does seem rather prolonged! It was all a bit hair-raising to begin with, although when I gave it some thought I realised that if I had missed all the wires and had had to go round again, the ramp would still have made the aircraft airborne over the lift and a bounce off the forward end would have been quite normal.

It so happened that, when I joined the ship, most of the Squadron were ashore at Hatston, so I left the ship next day and moved to the air station to meet the rest of the Squadron, and in particular the observer and TAG with whom I hoped to form an efficient and friendly crew.

Hatston was a wartime airfield and had none of the luxuries of the RAF peacetime aerodromes. The accommodation was adequate, if somewhat spartan, and the hangars, workshops, crewrooms and other facilities were what we had come to expect wherever we went. My first flying ashore was familiarisation with the aircraft again and getting to know the area as thoroughly as possible because there were no radio aids to help one to return to base in the event of poor visibility—and we had to avoid flying over the Fleet in Scapa Flow because the ship's gun crews were free to fire at anything appearing to threaten it.

I was surprised to be told that the main runway was in fact part of the main road from Kirkwall to the west of the island, two lanes wide and with a gate at each end. Of course, the runway was out of sight under the nose of the aircraft and I was not at all sure that I could stay on the road during take-off. However, all was well and I fairly quickly got used to it while we practised anti-submarine attacks, during the course which I flew with a number of different observers and TAGs, with the result that I did not form a particular crew as I had expected.

After a week of this, we embarked in *Furious* to form part of the protection for one of the Murmansk convoys. My first operational flight was an anti-submarine strike against a U-boat which had been reported off the coast of Norway north of Tromsø. It was a lovely day with good visibility, and my observer said he felt that we would have a wasted trip as 'they will see us coming from miles away and be fully submerged.' He was right. Although we searched around the reported position for as long as our briefed time allowed, we saw nothing and set off back to our moving base, aiming to be at the expected position in time to land-on with other returning aircraft. After about an hour we arrived at the rendezvous—and not a ship was in sight. Of course, we had to maintain radio silence and I was getting very worried, wondering what I had done wrong. Luckily, my observer was older and much more experienced and he calmed me and suggested that we start a square search. On the fifth leg, I saw a smudge of smoke in the distance, so we abandoned the search and set off in that direction. I was so relieved to find that it was *Furious* and her escort belting along at high speed (which was lucky for us, because at normal cruising speed naval vessels made very little smoke). I never did find out the reason for the carrier abandoning her intended line of advance: I was just happy to have landed-on safely because our fuel was getting just a bit too low.

The ship returned to Scapa and we flew ashore again to Hatston. I was rather surprised to discover that some of the older aircrew did not disembark in their flying suits: they wore their uniforms and, on one particular occasion, a greatcoat on top! It appeared that the normal drill on returning to Hatston from the ship was to fly over the air station—twelve aircraft in echelon starboard—before breaking to land in quick succession. As one of those on the 'whiplash' end of the echelon, I found it to be another of my many hair-raising experiences.

We found that the Squadron had been selected to carry out 'B' bombing attacks. The 'B' bomb was a buoyant device and the idea was to drop a stick of four ahead of a ship at sea, across its intended line of advance: the bombs would sink to a specified depth, then rise back and strike the ship in its least heavily armoured area. The weapon had an explosive charge of 250 pounds (I think) carried inside an elongated-oval-shaped flotation tank designed to bring the weapon back to the surface. The theory was that at least one of the bombs would strike the ship, even if the latter altered course during the attack.

It seemed odd to me that no one gave us any details of how long it would take the bomb to travel from dropping height to reach its deepest point and then float back to the surface. This time period was absolutely essential information for us because we needed to judge how far ahead of the ship to aim. After all, we would have to be able to estimate how fast the ship was travelling, then guess the aiming point using the length of the ship as a measure of the distance—some fairly intricate mental arithmetic whilst being fired at by people determined to knock you out of the sky!

From my point of view—and admittedly I had no operational experience at all at that time—it seemed that the system had been thought up by Heath Robinson himself, and so unlikely to succeed as to be a total waste of time, money and effort. In all, I flew eighteen sorties, the final two with dummy bombs against a live target, HMS *Swiftsure*. I often wondered what the target ship's company thought about that particular lark: I suspect that they must have had fairly dark thoughts about Their Lordships exposing them to the tender mercies of youngsters like me. Luckily there were no mishaps, but I never found out whether the bombs had surfaced anywhere near the target or whether they had disappeared, never to be heard of again. As far as I am aware, the 'B' bomb was never developed as a serious weapon for use by the Pacific Fleet.

Rugged, Complex and Capable *Commander Bertie Vigrass OBE VRD*

My squadron, 810, was the first operational squadron equipped with Barracuda aircraft to embark in an aircraft carrier and to go into action. The date was September 1943, the ship was HMS *Illustrious* and the action was Operation 'Avalanche', the Allied invasion of Italy at Salerno. 810 was a battle-hardened squadron having been based on board *Illustrious* for the previous eighteen months in the Eastern Fleet flying Swordfish and taking part in Operation 'Ironclad', the invasion of Madagascar at Diego Suarez, and also in operations against the Japanese along the coast of Burma. I was a member of the Squadron throughout this period.

Following her deployment to the Indian Ocean, the ship returned to the Clyde in March 1943 and the Squadron was disembarked to Machrihanish. We were informed that we were to be re-equipped with Barracudas and that six weeks had been allocated for the pilots to learn to fly the aircraft, to work-up and to be ready to re-embark in *Illustrious*. This was a challenge we accepted with enthusiasm.

Our conversion started with a week at RAF Errol during which we were provided with six flights in a Miles Master, one in a Hawker Hurricane and two in a Barracuda Mk I. We then moved to Lee-on-Solent to receive our Barracuda IIs. We found Lee a great place for our work-up: the Stokes Bay range was available for our simulated and actual torpedo dropping exercises, Thorney Island was available for night flying and Lee-on-Solent was ideal for ADDLs (Aerodrome Dummy Deck Landings).

We were of course aware of the problems being experienced by other squadrons trying to form with the Barracuda. However, we did not allow this to deflect us from our task. We continued to use our well established method of carrying out torpedo attacks. We would put the aircraft into a steep dive from around 8,000 feet with the air brakes out and pull out of the dive at around 500 feet to enable us to drop the torpedo at 200 feet at about 200 knots. The major problem was the violent nose-down change of trim about seven seconds after the dive brakes had been retracted, but we were always prepared for this and ready to take appropriate action. The other problem was the very powerful elevator trimmer which, if used to excess when pulling out of a steep dive, could risk overstraining the aircraft. I always took great care when using this trimming tab. We lost one pilot who crashed into the sea at Stokes Bay when carrying out simulated torpedo attacks: he may have been caught out by violent change of trim problems.

On 21 May the Squadron, having made very good progress, flew to Machrihanish to be ready for re-embarkation. On 8 April I was detailed to fly out to the ship, and after landing on—this was, of course, my first Barracuda deck landing—I was told that my task for the day was to carry out catapult and arrester-wire trials in advance of the arrival of the Squadron. During the day I completed fourteen launches and landings with a wide variety of loads on the aircraft—one 250-pound bomb, then two bombs, then three bombs, then four, and then, on seven launches, a torpedo. By the end of the day I was an experienced Barracuda deck-landing pilot!

The ship left the Clyde and joined the Home Fleet. In July she took part of a major diversionary operation off Norway before sailing to the Mediterranean to join Force H and to take part in the invasion at Salerno. When the ship

Below: Spot on! The writer—a very experienced naval pilot—considered the Barracuda to be the easiest type of aircraft to land, prior to the introduction of modern deck-landing aids. This is a standard Mk II having just landed on; notice the ever-watchful planeguard destroyer keeping station off the port quarter. The light patch around the Barracuda's main intake appears to be a flaw in the photograph rather than airframe paintwork.

Right: Despite most pilots' high opinion of the Barracuda as a deck landing aircraft, there were, inevitably, 'incidents', as illustrated by this unconventional arrival on board the training carrier HMS *Rajah*. The port main undercarriage of this 767 Squadron aircraft has collapsed, and the pilot is at the mercy of Fate (although such events were not often injurious). The arrester hook is clearly seen, and, again, notice the handling struts deployed to aid the deck crew.

returned to the Clyde in November 1943, I left her, and the Squadron, to take up a new appointment of Barracuda deck-landing training instructor with 769 Squadron at RNAS East Haven. Six months later I was appointed Commanding Officer of 767 Squadron, the other Barracuda deck-landing training unit at East Haven. In the spring of 1945 I completed the School of Naval Air Warfare Course at St Merryn and was appointed CO of 818 Squadron, my task being to form this new Squadron as a torpedo bomber reconnaissance unit equipped with Barracuda IIs, which was intended for the 22nd Carrier Air Group in a *Colossus* class aircraft carrier. We completed our work-up at RNAS Rattray and moved to RNAS Fearn, and we were on embarkation leave when 'the bomb' was dropped and the war in the Far East ended. My last wartime task was to disband No 818 Squadron.

This brought to an end my day-to-day involvement with the Barracuda, which had extended over a period of two and a half years. Pilots seemed to have very strong views about the aircraft. Some took a great dislike to it and did all they could to avoid flying it, but, for my part, I accepted it as a rugged and complex aircraft, capable of carrying out the task for which it had been designed. I quite enjoyed flying it.

My deck-landing days preceded the introduction of the angled deck and the mirror landing sight, of course. I had experience of deck-landing quite a number of different types of naval aircraft, however, from the Swordfish to the Seafire 17. As far as the Barracuda was concerned I had no problems. The view from the cockpit very good throughout the approach, the aircraft was steady and, with everything down, the high level of boost needed to counter the drag meant that when the throttle was closed at the 'cut', the aircraft dropped like a stone and remained glued to the deck. I rate the Barracuda as one of the easiest naval aircraft to deck-land during the years in which I served.

Below: The duty runway at RNAS East Haven, home to 731, 767 and 769 Squadrons in 1943-45, was controlled as if it were the flight deck of an aircraft carrier. 'HMS Spurious', a very large van modified to look like the island of a carrier, was located on the right-hand side of the runway, just ahead of the touch-down zone for landing aircraft. This arrangement made ADDLs more realistic, and greater concentration was required on the part of the pilot. Even visiting aircraft were expected to do a circuit at 200 feet and to be 'batted in'. Here Barracudas, with a few Seafires and Sea Hurricanes bringing up the rear, have been ranged as for a mass strike.

No Guns in Anger Petty Officer (A) Arthur Wells MiD

I joined up as a 'Hostilities Only' entrant into the Royal Navy, volunteering as a telegraphist air gunner, on 8 September 1942 at HMS *Royal Arthur*, Skegness (Ingoldmells)—the temporarily evacuated Butlin's holiday camp—where, in company with some fifty others, I completed a six-week course in 'Ordinary Seaman' training. This included basics such as naval discipline, marching and oarsmanship, and of course we were kitted out. From Skegness we went to HMS *St Vincent* (Gosport), where, at the next level, we covered such classroom topics as Morse code training, aircraft and ship identification and gunnery. On completion of this stage of training, about half of 45 TAGs' Course—about forty of us, including me—were dispatched to Canada. With no time to say farewell to our families, we went by train to transit camp at Dunfermline before boarding the RMS *Andes* at Glasgow, and we set sail almost immediately. We arrived in Halifax, Nova Scotia, on Christmas Eve 1942. We were quickly kitted out with winter clothing, and then it was off to RCAF Yarmouth, where we would really get to grips with TAG training.

It was here that the flying began, in March, mostly in Swordfish but on occasion in Ansons, in order to put our training into practice. Our skills in ship and aircraft recognition, communications (importantly, Morse speeds and working with the Aldis lamp), wireless theory, gunnery (including cine gun operations) and, for some reason, semaphore (!) were practised and honed. The experience alone was quite wonderful: aside from the work itself, few if any of us—and we were all aged about eighteen—had ever before left Britain, and we were marvellously looked after both by the RCAF and by the civilian population. The weather at this time of the year was still harsh for flying around in open cockpits—we even experienced an ice storm on one occasion—but our enthusiasm and enjoyment was never once dampened. My flying time during training totalled 80 hours 50 minutes. I cannot overemphasise the warmth of the comradeship that resulted from our time spent training together: strong friendships were formed, which are still maintained to this day—although, sadly but inevitably, our numbers are rapidly dwindling.

Below: TAGs during training at Yarmouth, Nova Scotia, March 1943. The writer is seated to the right of the photograph.

In late September 1943, having travelled through Canada and the United States by train to New York, we joined the RMS *Queen Mary*, now a troopship, and after a typical American send-off, all bands marching and flags, again crossed the Atlantic, unescorted, to disembark at Glasgow. We then enjoyed two weeks' leave.

It was the beginning of October when I was drafted to HMS *Dædalus* (RNAS Lee-on-Solent), having successfully completed the course and been awarded my 'wings' (somewhat perfunctorily handed out by the course tutor, as seemed to be the procedure for TAGs!). After a few weeks I received a draft chit to Scapa Flow and HMS *Furious*, where in November I joined 830 Squadron, flying Barracudas, shore-based at RNAS Hatston and, with 827 Squadron, making up No 8 TBR Wing. I had never seen a Barracuda before, let alone flown in one! We TAGs had a wonderful Petty Officer, Jan Lock, and he introduced me to the delights and complications of the Barracuda—which had guns and radio equipment that I had never come across. I became intimately associated with the aircraft—all the more quickly since, as *Furious*'s TAGs' Mess was overcrowded, there was no room for me there and I spent the nights in a hammock slung beneath one of them in the hangar!

The Barracuda TAG's cockpit was cramped, and access was awkward. It was difficult to open the hood in flight and to deploy the guns. I'm thankful that I never had to fire in anger—by the time we gunners could retaliate the threat would have long since disappeared. As well as the weapons and their ammunition, and all the communications equipment (radio, Morse key, Aldis lamp, etc.), we looked after the Very pistol and also the flares, the latter attached to the sides of the cockpit and discharged down the chute beneath us as and when required. VHF radio began to be introduced for the pilots' use at about this time, but we TAGs were concerned only with W/T. 'My' aircraft was LS576, with the side number '5G' painted red with a white outline.

I was extremely fortunate in having a splendid pilot and observer—respectively, Sub-Lieutenants Des Rowe RNZVR and David Brown RNZVR (the latter went on to become a well-known naval historian and author). They treated me as an equal—not the experience of many TAGs. One particular memory is of waking up (still in the hammock!) on New Year's Eve to discover somebody rocking the bedding. My initial reaction was not entirely polite, but after rubbing my eyes I saw Des Rowe and David Brown standing there with a cake that had been sent from New Zealand. They wanted me to share it with the rest of the boys in the Mess.

Our back-up was absolutely first class. We had our own personal aircraft engineer (known to all as 'Ginger'), and also our own armourer, who looked after the guns etc., and rigger for the airframe. We TAGs had the responsibility to check that our guns were in proper working order, but we relied upon the ground crews to maintain everything in top condition—which they did. We were very lucky, and, needless to say, we had absolute confidence in them.

Over the next few weeks and months the ship was in and out of Scapa Flow on exercises. My logbook records such events as '28 January—First use of twin guns . . . Results poor (!)'. My first operation took place on 11 February, when we flew off the carrier to Statlandet, north of Bergen in Norway, where we 'bombed a beached ship and left it on fire'. On that occasion my pilot was Sub-Lieutenant Britton RNVR. Then we had the 'big one'—Operation 'Tungsten' (the attack on the German battleship *Tirpitz*), which my colleague Robert McCandless has covered in some depth elsewhere in this book. On 26 April we attacked merchant shipping off Bodø, and we mounted a similar raid off Kristiansand on 6 May. On 15 May we were hoping to return to attack *Tirpitz* (Operation 'Brawn') but didn't, owing to bad weather. On 1 June we returned again to Statlandet, dive-bombing shipping, following which operation Captain Philip took the fleet very near the coast, in what we later learned to be a feint preparatory to D-Day five days later. D-Day itself, 6 June, came and went, but we remained at Hatston and, flying from *Furious*, continued our operations in northern waters. On 7 July No 8 TBR Wing took part in another operation against *Tirpitz* ('Mascot'), but on this occasion we were unsuccessful as the enemy's defensive smokescreen was too effective. After further exercises, including participation in 'Goodwood', I left *Furious* at the end of September, via Thurso by train en route to Suffolk.

827 Squadron, on which I was now serving, flew to RAF Beccles in October and then Langham, sharing the facilities with the RAF, but did not fly on offensive operations, continuing instead with working-up exercises with the new crew members. On 22 November we moved to Machrihanish to begin training for our deployment to the Far East. The weather restricted our flying—there was none in December and there were only four flights in January. By the middle of the month we had joined HMS *Colossus*, one of the new light fleet aircraft carriers, and by the end of January we had flown to RAF Ballyhalbert to continue our work-up.

Although our ship and shore bases had changed from when I first joined just over a year previously, the TAG's duties were the same as before. Very shortly after arriving in Northern Ireland, however, I was drafted to RNAS Lee-on-Solent, and, although still flying Barracudas, was now not attached to a squadron, instead carrying out general TAG duties. At the end of August 1945 I moved to RNAS Hinstock (HMS *Godwit*), near Stretton, to join the Naval Advanced Instrument Flying School. Here we flew Oxfords: my days as a Barracuda TAG had ended. The last time I flew was 7 December 1945, having amassed a grand total of 330 hours 50 minutes' day flying and 7 hours 25 minutes' night—all as a TAG.

Above: The personnel of one of 830 Squadron's Flights in front of one of *Furious*'s 'pompom' mountings, May 1944. Des Rowe is seated far left, David Brown is standing second from left, and Arthur Wells is to the latter's right.

Below: A photograph of HMS *Furious*, probably taken in the spring of 1942, soon after she had completed a refit at Philadelphia; she remained substantially unaltered for the rest of her days. The writer describes her as a very 'happy ship', despite her cramped conditions—she had been completed as a large cruiser but now had to accommodate some 1,200 souls, half as many again as originally catered for—and recalls that the high morale was due in no small part to the personality of her Captain during his time on board, Captain G. T. Philip DSO DSC RN. As an example of the Captain's propensity to waive 'the rules', after the 'Tungsten' operation he issued an invitation to all TAGs to join him and his aircrew officers in the Wardroom for dinner. In the Navy this sort of thing was virtually unheard of—TAGs were, of course, 'lower deck'. In the photograph, the dark scar on the forward edge of the flight deck is where the wartime censor has deleted the forward high-angle gun director and its radar array.

Waiting for Vengeance *Lieutenant (A) John Dickson* RD RNVR

My Squadron, 812, was re-formed at RNAS Stretton (HMS *Blackcap*) on 1 June 1944, initially with twelve Barracudas which later increased to sixteen. Our CO was Lieutenant-Commander (A) C. R. J. Coxon RN, who was, at the time, the youngest lieutenant-commander in the Royal Navy (I believe he was only 23). He had already had a busy war in Malta and had been Mentioned in Dispatches. The original complement of aircrew was CO Cedric Coxon, Lieutenant Peter Poole (Senior Pilot), Lieutenant 'Poppa' Bristow, Lieutenant Charlie Wintringham RNZNVR, Sub-Lieutenants Les Terry, Digby and 'Jock' Balfour, Midshipman 'Dicky' Dickson and Acting Petty Officers Steve Blakey, 'Slip' Slater and Sid Hunt. There were also six pilots—Sub-Lieutenants D. S. (Sam) Smallwood, Pete ('Ace') Throssel, Dick ('Robbie') Burns, Jack ('Jackie') Birch, 'Happy' Pain and Johnny Cookson—who had recently returned from the United States, where they had been trained and where they had flown SBD Dauntless dive bombers, the aircraft that had acquitted themselves so well at the Battle of Midway. The Royal Navy had acquired some Curtiss Helldiver dive bombers (a more modern aircraft) and formed 1820 Squadron. It was intended to form other squadrons, and our six lads thought that that was where they would go. However, the Helldivers were *lethal*! 1820 Squadron soon packed up (and, I believe, the aircraft were too big for our ships in any case). Nonetheless our six 'Yankee' trained boys were not happy bunnies when they discovered that their destiny was Barracudas.

There was a nucleus of senior (or experienced) observers with us from the outset—Lieutenants 'Spike' Regan (Senior Observer), Gordon ('Blood') Wallace and 'Toby' Tobias, and Sub-Lieutenant 'Tommy' Dewsnap. I am not sure how many telegraphist air gunners were in our original complement, probably eight or nine. I know Petty Officer Casey (Senior TAG), Rouse, Hughes, Sargent and Geoff Squire were among them, as was Petty Officer 'Pip' Piper.

When we 'clocked on' on 1 June, most of us pilots had not flown Barracudas, so we hustled across the airfield to 798 Squadron, where we had an intensive conversion course by way of Masters, Fulmars and, finally Barracudas themselves. After six trips on 'Barras' I was back with 812, and I first flew with the Squadron on 17 June.

In those days it was normal for aircrew to do their operational training as individuals in the various training schools around the country. Torpedo attacks, dive bombing, anti-submarine attacks, target spotting and deck landing were all taken step by step, and, when these had been completed, the pilots were matched up with observers and air gunners who had been similarly engaged with their own trades. As fully integrated crews, they then waited in a 'pool' until they were fed into the operational squadrons as demanded and on a piecemeal basis.

We were different: probably as guinea pigs, we carried out all this operational training as a coherent squadron—and I think it worked. Morale was high, we got to know one another really well and there is no doubt that we were pretty good! This system also gave the CO and the Senior Observer the opportunity to weed out the few who were not going to measure up. Although we did not know it for some months, we had already been earmarked for one of the new light fleet carriers, which were expected to be ready from late October. 814 Squadron (who went to HMS *Venerable*) worked up in similar fashion although they did not form until 1 July 1944—so we were the first and the best! I think that 837 (destined for *Glory*, as one might say) were the only other Barracuda squadron to be trained in this manner.

On 28 June 1944 we left Stretton bound for RNAS Crail (HMS *Jackdaw*) on the northern side of the Firth of Forth. We stayed there until 7 September and our time was spent learning torpedo attack—day and night—A/S bombing and W/T exercises. It was all very intensive, quite scary at times and hard work. Cedric Coxon led us brilliantly. Amazingly, by March 1945, when we were in Malta, we were told to forget all about torpedo attack—there were no enemy ships left to sink! After that we were concerned mainly with dive bombing, anti-submarine work and army co-operation duties.

Steve Blakey must have been quick off the mark when we got to Crail. He found himself a girlfriend who lived at Lochton Farm, some six miles from the airfield. On 13 July he was showing her how low he could fly when he forgot the sloping ground and crashed into a field on the farm. Sadly Leading Airman Sargent, his TAG, was in the back and they were both killed. I remember, as a nineteen-year-old, being upset (Steve had been on the next course to me while training), but Cedric was really livid. In his eyes Steve had broken all the rules, he was showing off, and he had killed another crew member and written off an aircraft He had no sympathy, and on reflection he was right. The funerals took place in the churchyard at Crail. Cedric would not let me go—he was obviously trying to protect someone so young. Apart from Sam Smallwood bending his aircraft in a landing accident, we completed our time at Crail without further incident and proved ourselves to be highly competent torpedo pilots.

On 7 September we left Crail in formation and flew down to RNAS Burscough (HMS *Ringtail*), just inland from Southport. On the way Les Terry, in LS841, had problems with the fuel feed and he ditched very gently off Blackpool Tower, he and Dewsnap stepping off the sinking aircraft into the dinghy and barely getting their feet wet. Dewsnap was delighted—he was going on leave to get married and had with him a new uniform (which had also stayed dry). Robbie Burns followed them down, and when he knew they were okay he landed at Squires Gate as he was, by then, low on fuel. Many years later I learned that the Lytham St Annes Lifeboat, which picked them up, chalked up its one and only rescue mission. It was never again called out during the war.

At Burscough a whole crowd of newly qualified and recently commissioned observers waited anxiously as news of what had just happened filtered through. There were some pale and apprehensive faces when we met. These

Above: A 'prang' involving an 812 Squadron Barracuda, MX737, on board *Vengeance*, the result of the starboard undercarriage leg having collapsed as the aircraft was landing. This incident occurred on 21 February 1945, during the Squadron's extensive work-up preparatory to deployment to the Far East. The pilot was Sub-Lieutenant Ashton.

observers had been pupils of 'Blood' Wallace when he was an instructor at Arbroath, and we understood that he had picked the best of the course to come to 812. There was one midshipman among them—'Bambi' Brook (who looked too young to have left his mother)—so he was allocated to me. Geoff Squire, our TAG, was somewhat older, and certainly more worldly-wise. It was generally accepted that he was our father figure and the boss of the show. Geoff was a wonderful swimmer and as strong as an ox. I felt happy with him in the back seat because I was a very poor swimmer and tended to keep my Mae West partly inflated—just in case. Geoff was courting an Admiral's daughter at that time, which just went to show that you didn't need a commission in order to impress the ladies!

We stayed at Burscough until 10 November 1944, mainly doing observer-type exercises—navexes, W/T etc.—though we still did some torpedo practice (some at night), dive bombing and fighter evasion. A new game involved 'corkscrewing' in formation while being 'attacked' by the Fireflies of 1772 Squadron. On 6 October I was doing an air test in a Barracuda, got up to 10,000 feet and managed to loop the aircraft. Some said that it couldn't be done, but I enjoyed it and it soon showed the crew that it was really quite safe. I was told that someone else (probably Throssel) had managed to roll a Barracuda, but I never tried it.

On 19 October Peter Poole said it was time for us to practice deck landing. The exercise ADDLs (Aerodrome Dummy Deck Landings) involved a tight, low circuit, a slow approach just above the stall with plenty of power on, and following the batsman's signals down to the deck, where, one hoped, he gave the 'cut', when you chopped power and sank gracefully on to the runway. Then, without stopping, you picked up the flaps, opened up and went round to do it again . . . and again . . . and again . . . When doing this in order to give the batsman practice, we became known as 'clockwork mice'. We were a bit apprehensive: no one likes dragging in just above the stall speed, and we were even more in wonder when Peter said, 'We'll make a start straight away—like *tonight*!' Thus it was that I did my first ADDLs at night. Having survived the first landing, I opened up my aircraft, LS752, to go round again, but in my panic I pulled the flap lever right through a little gate to the dive-brake position. Since Barracudas would not get airborne with the dive brakes on, I ended up in the hedge at the end of the runway. No one was hurt and the aircraft was barely scratched, but I had learned a lesson.

We left Burscough for Fearn (HMS *Owl*, the most northerly Navy airfield on the mainland) on 10 November, by which time we were fully worked up and ready to go to sea— but no, the ship wasn't ready and they had to send us somewhere. My logbook shows a three-hour flight, and my memory is of cold, snowy and frosty weather, a pretty bleak airfield and no nearby town where one could enjoy a good run ashore. So we continued the usual grind—A/S bombing, dive bombing, navexes, search-and-rescue exercises, fighter evasion with Seafires, and so on. The airfield was pretty crowded: 814 and 837 Squadrons were also there, all, like us, ready and waiting to join carriers that were delayed. Peter Poole taxied into the mud and got stuck. We practised carrier ranging—pretending to be on a flight deck and being flagged of in quick succession, then joining formation with two other Barracuda squadrons. It must have looked impressive.

On 25 November 1944 we had our worst day. We were to take off on one of these carrier ranging exercises. It was very cold and very frosty, and apart from being iced up I couldn't get my aircraft started. This meant a delay while new cartridges were installed. Meanwhile the rest of the Squadron took off and my position in the first sub-flight was empty. Hunt and Muncer, flying LS679 and MD646, both thought they would fill the slot, although as far as I

69

know no orders were given for either of them to do so. One came in from below and one from above (pilots should *never* do this!), so one aircraft just sat on top of the other. Both fell into Nigg Bay. Five of the six crewmen died and Harry Saggs escaped with a broken back. Of course, on hearing the news we were all in a state of shock and disbelief. There was a postscript to this tragedy, with a happier outcome. While attending Muncer's funeral near Leeds, CO Cedric Coxon met 'Bonny', a friend of the family and herself a widow. They married in February the following year, and remained together for over forty years before 'Bonny' passed away.

Meanwhile, back at Fearn, life carried on and we all became rather bored. Exercises were repeated over and over and social life was almost non-existent. Christmas came and went. The Scottish New Year was a bit livelier, although there was a grave shortage of Wrens. We were becoming rather a nuisance as Fearn was getting overcrowded. Other Squadrons in a less advanced state of working-up needed our quarters, but where to send us? Eventually we were offered space at RAF Ballyhalbert (later RNAS Ballyhalbert, HMS *Corncrake*) in Northern Ireland.

On 5 January 1945, in Squadron formation (now eighteen aircraft), we flew from Fearn to Ballyhalbert. This was a forlorn and desolate spot: cold, snow, ice, sleet and mud, and damp, miserable Nissan huts, which probably hadn't been used for months, to sleep in. Our 'landlords' the RAF, were not at all friendly or hospitable. Most of us were so cold at night we didn't bother to undress. Carrier drill, dive bombing, A/S bombing and ADDLs were the order of the day. Sub-Lieutenant Hodgkinson retracted MX685's wheels instead of its flaps while taxying and Sub-Lieutenant Johnny Cookson in MD740 ran off the runway into the mud and stood the aircraft on its nose. No casualties.

At last, on 15 January 1945, HMS *Vengeance* was commissioned, and it was only then that we knew for sure that she was to be 'our' ship. Some of the crews 'walked' on board on the 25th, while the following day the rest of us (twelve aircraft) flew as a Squadron to the ship sailing off the Isle of Arran—where we made our first deck landing! I was in DR267. There were no accidents, and the drinks were free in the wardroom that night. The next day I did my first deck take-off and made my second deck landing, this time with full crew aboard. Remarkable! I think the 'back seat boys' were very brave.

Johnny Cookson, in 'my' aircraft, DR267, ended up half over the side on 27 January and the next day 'Poppa' Bristow did the same in LS850. There were no casualties, but two Barracudas were badly bent. On 1 February five aircraft flew off to Ballyhalbert to collect odds and ends left ashore. On the way back to the ship, the weather closed right down and we got split up. Flying in nil visibility and mindful of the high ground on the Mull of Kintyre, I turned back to Ballyhalbert and two or three others did likewise. The rest pressed on at sea level and squeaked into RNAS Ayr (HMS *Wagtail*), where I joined them the next day. It was a complete shambles and could have been very tragic. We were stuck at Ayr until the weather cleared, and we able to fly back to the ship on 4 February.

On 10 February Sub-Lieutenant Alfie Fyles (LS862) tangled with the barrier while landing on but only the aircraft was hurt. At that time Sub-Lieutenant Jack Birch and I flew off to Ayr, and for the next week we were guests of Rolls-Royce in Derby on an engine-handling course. We lived in luxury and enjoyed a good break. The ship was at anchor off Greenock when we reported back on board on 17 February.

The boys from 1850 Squadron flew aboard in their Corsairs on 25 February, having previously done some deck landings on HMS *Venerable*. I had lost another of my aircraft (mine were usually coded 'R') on 21 February when Ashton landed MX737 heavily on the deck and the undercarriage collapsed. No one was hurt. We were making a mess of the Barracudas, because Sub-Lieutenant Rushbrook (another New Zealander) flew PM762 into the barrier at night on 1 March and three days later Lieutenant Charlie Wintringham RNZNVR with Sub-Lieutenant 'Shiner' Wright in the back stalled PM813 on approach and flopped into the sea astern of the ship. They were quickly fished out.

We sailed for Gibraltar on 12 March 1945, having spent the odd day at Ayr when I flew a couple of trips to RNAS Abbotsinch (HMS *Sanderling*) collecting replacement aircraft. En route to Gibraltar there was a U-boat scare and we flew the odd A/S patrol. (Operational at last!) Nothing was seen, but believe it or not this qualified us for the Atlantic Star service medal. We did not go ashore in Gibraltar but soon passed into the Mediterranean, where on the 20th we flew off the ship to RNAS Hal Far (HMS *Falcon*).

On 24 March, 'Jock' Balfour damaged his undercarriage doing ADDLs in PM745. Night dive bombing and night A/S bombing on towed targets were new games and good fun. Otherwise we practised laying mines in Tripoli harbour and on Lampedusa Island. We dropped bombs on Filfla rock, which, we were assured, was uninhabited. On 4 April Sub-Lieutenant Hodgkinson's engine failed and he ditched into a calm sea. He, Sub-Lieutenant 'Dicky' Boston and their TAG were soon picked up by the air–sea rescue launch, a bit wet but unhurt—but one less Barracuda remained. In less than a week tragedy struck again. On 6 April Sub-Lieutenant Bardner, one of our Corsair pilots, baled out some way off the coast after his engine failed. His parachute was seen to open and the position was pretty well marked. During the day we flew off searches, feeling certain that we would see him in his dinghy, but no one did. I think we all volunteered to fly again that night hoping to see some signal flares from the dinghy. The sea was quite calm and it was a cloudless night. I took off in PM750 at about the same time as Jack Birch in MX783; we were to fly diverging courses to the search area. No more was ever heard of Jack and his crew, Sub-Lieutenant Dave Robins and Petty Officer Hamill. No wreckage was ever seen, no

Right: 'In the drink': Sub-Lieutenant Hodgkinson's Barracuda PM854, having been forced to ditch off Malta, is abandoned by its crew, all three of whom are visible preparing to board the aircraft's dinghy (the white 'disc' on the starboard side), which the TAG is attending to. Because the aircraft was nose-heavy thanks to its Merlin engine, the pilot required a little more alacrity in escaping than his colleagues: he is already standing on the wing. The position of the external lanyard for releasing the dinghy was indicated by the sinuous white stripe painted on the port side of the aft fuselage that is so evident in photographs of Barracudas.

one knew what caused the accident, and the Corsair pilot was never found either.

A few new crews had joined the Squadron just before we left Britain and now we picked up three more. By this time we had a total complement of eighteen Barracudas. At the same time a few 'old hands' departed the scene, notably 'Blood' Wallace, our second Senior Observer. At about this time there was some disquiet over the structural strength of the Barracuda, metal fatigue being mentioned. Apart from ours there had been other unexplained crashes, and so, in rotation, our aircraft were withdrawn and, where necessary, the wing spars and cross sections were strengthened. There were also rumours that we would be re-equipping with Avengers, but I doubt if this was ever an option as there were no aircraft to spare and the light fleet carriers were not designed to operate these larger and heavier machines.

On 1 May I suffered my one and only deck landing accident. After I had taken off from the ship in PM750 my throttle lever jammed (it was later discovered to be a linkage problem), which meant that I could not fully close the throttle and which in turn would mean a fast approach. At the same time Geoff's gunner's hood had jammed open, and this would make control even more difficult at low speeds. The deck declared a full emergency and we nearly got away with it. We caught the last (eighth) wire but the barrier operator didn't quite get things lowered in time and the prop hit the barrier, although there was no other damage. It couldn't have been too bad because I flew the same aircraft three days later, although not without incident. It was a night take-off using the accelerator and this time the wheels would not come up, so we did a quick 'about turn' and landed back on board before the ship steered out of wind. All this happened in my own aircraft, coded 'N1R'. About a week earlier we were a bit upset with Les Terry. Taking off from the deck one night, he flew the aircraft immediately ahead of me. He failed to obey the rules, which were to turn smartly starboard on leaving the deck to clear the prop wash for the chap already on his way up the deck behind. When I went off the front end I had virtually no control and we rolled to starboard and slipped below deck level. Instinct and deliverance from on high gave me the strength to kick a full left rudder and somehow we missed the wave tops and staggered into the air. 'Bambi', Geoff and I thought Terry should pay our laundry bills for soiled underwear but he seemed quite unconcerned.

'Poppa' Bristow had a new routine on 4 May. Instead of his usual landing to port, where the batsman had to take smart evasive action, he thought he'd give the starboard side his attention. Unfortunately he landed MX682 a 'bit long' and clobbered the crane with his wing tip. There was not much damage but I think the crane came off best.

On VE-Day, 8 May 1945, the ship was in Grand Harbour and looked a treat with all the lights blazing. There was a party in the Sliema Club and we spent a couple of days sailing and swimming. It was great to hear all the church bells ringing across the island. In retrospect, I think our celebrations were a bit subdued, probably because we knew that any action that might involve us was further east and we did not know how long that would last. Our war was not yet over.

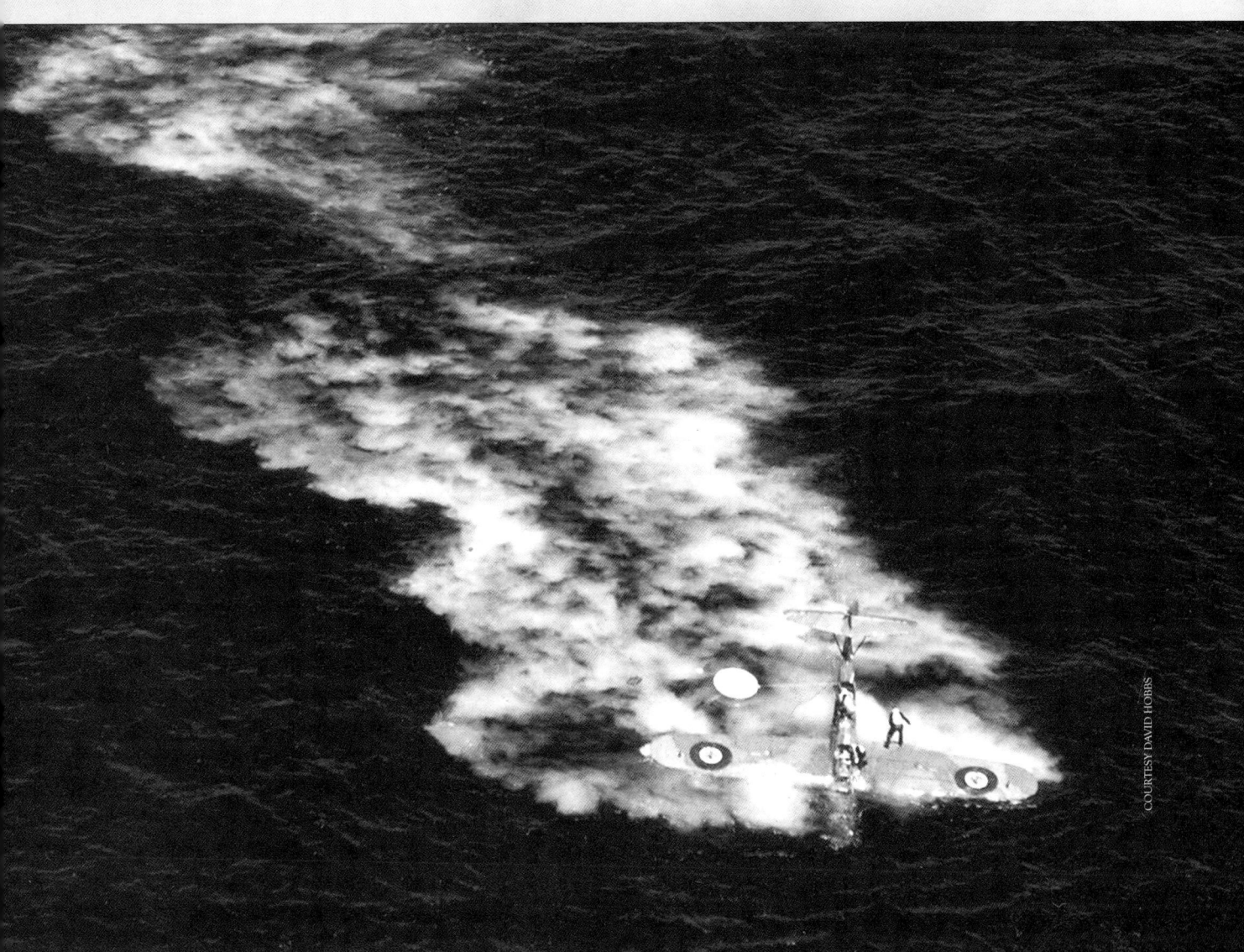

INTO ACTION

Lieutenant-Commander Robert McCandless DSC

THE Navy's planning over the previous months had brought them to the conclusion that we had mustered a very strong force and, provided we could find and see *Tirpitz*, there was a strong sense that an attack at this time could be successful. The actual timing was left to Vice-Admiral Sir Henry Moore (Second-in-Command Home Fleet). Of course, he was kept fully up to date with the photo-reconnaissance reports and the important information from the Norwegian agents.

The force which had been mustered comprised the battleship *Anson* (flagship of the force), the fleet carriers *Victorious* (24 Barracuda bombers and Corsair fighters) and *Furious* (18 Barracudas and Seafire fighters) and the escort carriers *Emperor* (Hellcat fighters), *Pursuer* (Wildcat fighters) and *Searcher* (Wildcat fighters). The attack was scheduled for 3 April.

Nos 8 Wing Barracudas and 52 Wing Barracudas split their aircraft between the two carriers *Victorious* and *Furious*, thus allowing each wing to get airborne and form up quickly in the first and second strikes, respectively. No 8 Wing, led by Lieutenant-Commander (A) Baker-Falkner and comprising 827 and 830 Squadrons, made up the twenty-one bombers of the first strike while No 52 Wing, led by Lieutenant-Commander (A) V. Rance and comprising 829 and 831 Squadrons, produced twenty bombers for the second strike.

The aircraft were loaded with a variety of bombs— AP and SAP, obviously, to try to penetrate the massive armour plating, MC bombs to try to destroy the superstructure and communications gear and A/S bombs to neutralise the light AA weapons or to damage the unarmoured parts of the hull in the

Below: Mounted on modified torpedo trolleys, 1,600-pound bombs are manœuvred on board one of the armoured carriers prior to a strike on the battleship *Tirpitz*, with two Barracudas and two Corsair fighters on hand. The photograph was probably taken during Operation 'Goodwood' (see text), which implies that the ship is HMS *Formidable*. The accompanying heavy cruiser is HMS *Berwick*.

Above: *Tirpitz* in her Norwegian hideout on 3 April 1944, apparently having weighed anchor. Smoke generators have recently been activated—to little effect, however, since the 'Tungsten' attack is mere seconds away.

event of a near-miss. Altogether, the two wings were loaded with ten 1,600-pound AP bombs, fifty-four 500-pound SAP, twenty-one 500-pound MC and four 600-pound A/S. It was planned for the first aircraft to attack to drop the MC and A/S weapons and most of those following to drop the AP and SAP bombs, and this did appear to be quite successful, but I get the impression that the reports of the damage caused by the fifteen hits convinced the squadron COs that subsequent attacks should use mainly the 1,600-pound AP.

April in the Arctic Circle is not a good time for operating aircraft from a carrier, and, to try to ensure 100 per cent serviceability, there was a considerable amount of activity overnight, moving aircraft up and down between the flight deck and hangar, warming up engines, final refuelling, etc., all the loading of bombs having been carried out the evening before. At four in the morning, all the hard work bore fruit: every aircraft started and, after engine testing, proved to be serviceable.

The take-off and join-up went according to plan and the 45 fighters forming the escort, from three different carriers, joined the bombers exactly as designed. They set off on a course of approximately 120 degrees in well-nigh perfect weather—a steady breeze of 12-14 knots from the south, maximum visibility, and very little by way of cloud over the coast.

The whole force flew low level to within about 25 miles of the coast, when they had to start climbing to allow the underpowered and loaded Barracudas to reach 10,000 feet, the best height for them to commence their attack. Everyone of the aircrews involved was very pleasantly surprised that there was no German air opposition. This meant that the low-level fighters were able to devote their attention to suppressing the flak and the bombers could make their attacks in copybook fashion.

It was obvious that everyone on the ground had been taken by surprise. There was no sign of life on any of the naval vessels in others parts of the fjord, and no anti-aircraft fire until the force was within three miles of the target. The smoke generators were not started until the aircraft were actually sighted—which, by that time, was much too late. The attack started at 0529 and was all over by 0530. All of the bombers saw two of the leader's three bombs explode on the ship, and this must have given them great encouragement and the confidence to know that they too had the opportunity to do the same. Sadly, one Barracuda was shot down. One Hellcat found himself with a damaged deck hook and the

Left, upper: First off: 830 Squadron's CO, Lieutenant-Commander R. D. Kingdon RNVR, with Lieutenant J. B. Armitage RNZNVR as observer and CPO A. E. Carr as TAG, takes off from HMS *Furious* in Barracuda '5A', armed with a 1,600-pound bomb, 3 April 1944. The photograph has received the attention of the wartime censor, who has deleted the ASV radar array. The 'Tungsten' strike comprised two waves, the first (Barracudas of 827 and 830 Squadrons) arriving at 0529 hours and the second (829 and 831) at 0635. Most of the Barracudas taking part appear to have had their fuselage codes painted red and outlined in white, but evidently not this one. Left, lower: Part of the 'Tungsten' strike force over the Norwegian fjords. The aircraft are about to deliver their attack on *Tirpitz*.

Captain decided that he should ditch rather than use the crash barrier lest a barrier incident escalate into an event which might block the flight deck for much longer and jeopardise the ship's ability to fulfil its planned part in the whole strike. The pilot was picked up by the destroyer *Algonquin*.

The second strike took off at 0525. One Barracuda failed to start and a second carried out a normal take-off but then crashed in the sea with the loss of the three aircrew. The approach to the target followed the same pattern as the first strike, but the aircrews could see from a long distance that the smokescreen more or less filled the fjord. Still there was no air opposition, only more concentrated flak, so once again the fighters went down first to suppress it as much as they could, and quite successfully too. By great good fortune, the bomber pilots were able to see the target, but the smoke must have hampered the view of the close range anti-aircraft crews. The box barrage put up by the ship and the heavy AA guns around the fjord was a defence measure whereby the gunnery control visualised a 'box' above the target through which the dive bombers would have to fly, and their intention was to try to fill this box with exploding shells by carefully controlling which piece of sky had to be targeted by which battery.

The sight of all these exploding shells as the aircraft approached the point where they had to start their dives was somewhat daunting, and, in fact, one Barracuda was shot down. Rear-Admiral I. G. W. Robertson CB DSC, a pilot on 827 Squadron at the time, recalls that 'on landing back . . . after the attack, my observer, the late Sub-Lieutenant McCormick, discovered that an enemy shell had come through the floor of his cockpit and passed between his legs and out through the Perspex top. Now that is what I call a near-miss!' No doubt the aircrew returning to the Fleet after the attacks—particularly the fighter aircrew, who did not have the benefit of observers as companions—were grateful for the presence en route of two destroyers which were there to pick out any men who had had to ditch and very helpfully pointed their main armament in the direction of home.

Altogether, the Barracudas claimed fifteen hits on the target and a number of near-misses, and, bearing in mind that four bombs were 'light case' and designed to wound hulls, who knows? There might have been serious underwater damage too.

Right: Two photographs taken on 3 April 1944 showing *Tirpitz* under attack by the Fleet Air Arm. Twenty hits were initially believed to have been scored by the combined force of 40 Barracudas (21 in the first wave and 20 in the second, but one aircraft from the latter crashed on take-off with the loss of all three aircrew); the Germans reported that the ship had suffered fifteen hits and two near-misses. In any event, *Tirpitz* had had her upperworks severely damaged and was disabled and rendered ineffective as a fighting unit. However, she had not been sunk, and this fact prompted further series of FAA operations over the ensuing months.

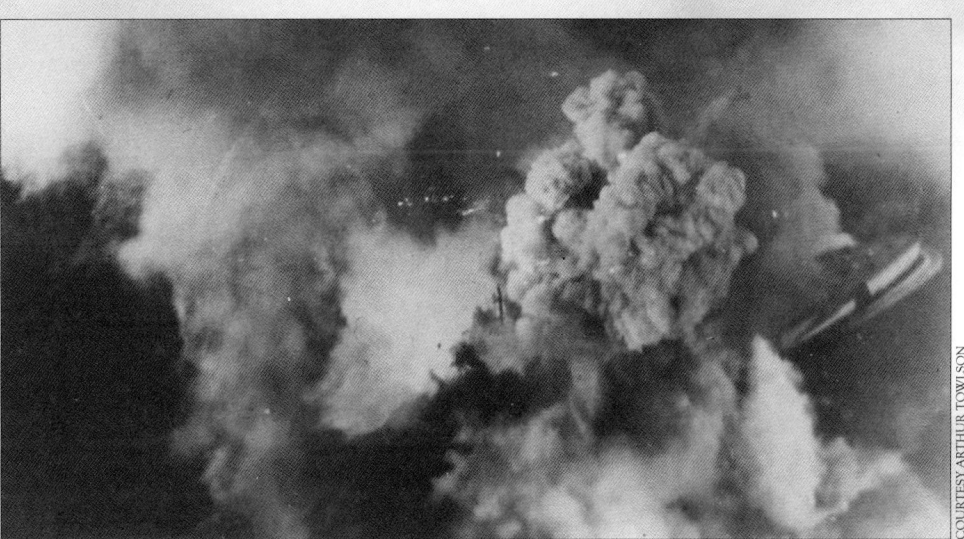

It appears that Vice-Admiral Moore had intended to repeat the attack next morning, but, having heard details of the damage inflicted, and also 'bearing in mind the fatigue of the aircrews and their natural reaction after completing a dangerous operation successfully,' he decided against it and sent everyone back to base. How little he knew about the young men of the Fleet Air Arm!

Although no damage had been done to *Tirpitz*'s main or auxiliary machinery, the near-misses—perhaps by the light-case A/S bombs—had caused flooding and the ship had developed a slight list, although this had been corrected by 6 April. The communications equipment was wrecked and the upper deck a complete shambles. A total of 121 men had been killed and 316 wounded, the latter including the Captain, many as a result of the fighter attacks. However, there is no doubt that the *Tirpitz* was a tough nut to crack: she was once again carrying out trials in Altenfjord just six weeks later.

Nevertheless, the Navy was determined to try to make sure that *Tirpitz* was put out of action permanently and a further series of attacks was planned, although the first three did not materialise: Operation 'Planet' (24 April 1944), involving forty Barracudas and forty escort fighters, was cancelled before take-off because of bad weather; 'Brawn' (15 May), involving twenty-seven Barracudas and thirty-six escort fighters, had also to be cancelled because of bad weather; and 'Tiger Claw' (18 May) was cancelled before any aircraft were launched.

Throughout the first half of July, prior to Operation 'Mascot', the Barracudas of the Fleet carried out a number of practice strikes on a target designated 'Port ZH'. This was in fact Loch Eriboll at Cape Wrath on the north-west corner of Scotland, and it had been chosen for a variety of reasons, not least because the target area was in an uninhabited mountainous region similar to that surrounding Altenfjord and Kaafjord. Moreover, Loch Eriboll was a narrow sea loch similar in size to Kaafjord, and it also had a small island close to one shore the shape and size of which offered the sort of aiming point we would have to use in earnest.

Another strike force was mustered in Scapa Flow with Admiral Moore, recently promoted to C-in-C Home Fleet, in the battleship *Duke of York* and his Deputy, Rear-Admiral R. R. McGrigor, on board the fleet carrier *Indefatigable*. They left harbour on 14 July in company with the carriers *Formidable* and

Furious. On this occasion *Furious* carried only six Swordfish for anti-submarine duties, twelve Seafires for Fleet protection and twenty Hellcats for escort and flak-suppression. *Indefatigable* had No 9 Wing (820 and 826 Squadrons) on board with twelve Barracudas each and 1770 Squadron with twelve Fireflies for escort and flak-suppression, while *Formidable* embarked No 8 Wing (827 and 830 Squadrons) with twelve Barracudas each, plus 1841 Squadron with eighteen Corsairs for escort and high cover.

The operation, dubbed 'Mascot', was planned for 17 July and the weather forecast was good. Forty-four Barracudas took part, all but two armed with 1,600-pound AP bombs and the other pair with 500-pound MCs. The weather remained fine until the aircraft reached the coast, when nearly half-cloud was encountered over Altenfjord. The smokescreen was already in place, and although this prevented the light AA gun crews within the fjord from seeing their targets all the positions on the surrounding hills had clear views and the heavy fire was already establishing a box barrage. Only two of the bombers and two fighters actually saw the target, albeit too briefly to be able to attack during the sighting, and all except four bombed through the smoke using the flashes of the big guns as their aiming points. The four aircrews who failed to drop on the target jettisoned their bombs on the way home. Two Barracudas ditched close to their carriers and the crews were picked up. A second strike had been planned, but this was cancelled when fog patches started to appear around the strike force.

Above: A Barracuda returns to HMS *Furious* following the 'Tungsten' attack on *Tirpitz*, 3 April 1944; two more Barracudas await their turn to land-on but they are not yet making their approach. Nothing unusual, one might think, but in fact there is: the aircraft touching down, 830 Squadron's LS576/'5G', piloted by Sub-Lieutenant D. E. Rowe, has a 'hang-up'—a 1,600-pound bomb that failed to release. Rowe spent some considerable time 'jinking' the aircraft in an effort to jettison the (unarmed) bomb over the sea, but when this proved impossible he was allowed to land on. Had the bomb become dislodged during the arrest, the theory would be that it would skim straight along the flight deck at 90 knots and disappear over the bow. In this photograph, the cruiser HMS *Belfast* is escorting off the starboard quarter.

Following the attack, *Tirpitz* reported no damage and only one near-miss; one Corsair was shot down and the pilot taken prisoner. Nevertheless, the Admiralty remained committed to the importance of dealing finally with the German battleship which so far had led such a charmed life thanks to the weather protection and, when the bombers had got through, to her own defences and armour, which had forestalled any permanent damage.

After the disappointing results of Operation 'Mascot', a fresh series of operations, code-named 'Goodwood', was planned for execution in the third week of August. It appears that the planners were concerned that the strike force might be subjected to air attack by the Luftwaffe during their three or four days remaining in the launching area in order to maintain the continuing series of strikes, and this concern was revealed in the make-up of the strike force. The principal ships, and their aircraft complements, were the fleet carriers *Indefatigable* (with twelve Barracudas of 820 Squadron, twelve Fireflies of 1770 Squadron and twelve Hellcats of 1840 for escort and flak-suppression, and sixteen Seafires from 887 and 894 Squadrons for fleet protection),

Formidable (twenty-four Barracudas from 826 and 828 and thirty Corsairs of 1841 and 1842 Squadrons, the latter aircraft mainly for top cover but also available for dive bombing in the absence of any German aircraft) and *Furious* (twelve Barracudas of 827 Squadron together with twenty-four Seafires of 801 and 880 Squadrons for fleet protection); and the escort carriers *Trumpeter* (with eight Avengers of 846 Squadron to lay mines across the entrance to Kaafjord and six Wildcats as escort and flak-suppression for the minelayers) and *Nabob* (with twelve Avengers from 852 Squadron to drop mines with various time-delay fuses and some immediate detonation, all to be dropped alongside *Tirpitz* in an attack to be synchronised with 846 Squadron, and four Wildcats flying in the escort and flak-suppression rôle). It was hoped that the mines being dropped close to the target might persuade *Tirpitz* to vacate her berth in Kaafjord and move out in Altenfjord, where the mines already laid by 846 Squadron might prove to be a more effective weapon against the unarmoured hull of the ship. Although the Squadron Commanders of the Avengers were of the opinion that the plan had some merit, privately they were doubtful about the survival rate when carrying it out in such a well-guarded area. In any case, if the smoke was thick, would the pilots of 852 Squadron even find the target to drop close to it? And, if they did manage to drop their mines, would *Tirpitz*'s commander realise what had been done and understand the threat if his ship were to remain at her berth?

The strike force left Scapa Flow on 18 August 1944 with the C-in-C on board *Duke of York* and his deputy in *Indefatigable*. The five carriers and three cruisers met their destroyers off the Faeroes. The first of the series of operations was planned for 21 August, but, once again 'the best-laid schemes o' mice an' men gang aft agley' and bad weather upset the timetable.

On the 22nd Admiral Moore decided to start the operation—known subsequently as 'Goodwood I'. It was intended to launch the aircraft at 0830, but this was delayed until 1100, when the Barracudas and the fighters took off. It was decided not to launch the Avengers because of the low cloud: if they had had to abort the operation because of conditions at Altenfjord, the mines they carried would have had to be ditched because pilots were forbidden to land

Below: Barracuda '5M', armed with a 1,600-pound bomb, takes off from HMS *Furious* for an attack on *Tirpitz* (probably one of the 'Goodwood' sorties in August 1944). A small extension to the ship's flight deck, in the form of a ramp over the rounded forward perimeter, was fashioned by *Furious*'s shipwrights to help the heavily laden aircraft get airborne. The camera appears to have caught the Barracuda during its customary take-off bounce!

back on board while still carrying them, and there were insufficient mines to enable a second attempt to be made.

As the Barracudas started to climb off the coast, thick cloud was encountered with its base at 1,500 feet. Thus, in accordance with the operational orders, the Barracudas and Corsairs returned to base. However, the Hellcats, Fireflies and Seafires continued at low level under the cloud and attacked targets of opportunity around the fjords. The Hellcats got as far as Kaafjord, where it was discovered that the cloud had broken up somewhat and they were able to drop their bombs from a relatively low level. One hit was claimed on *Tirpitz* and other ships around were also attacked, and on their return flight the aircrews claimed successful attacks on various installations and aircraft. In fact, *Tirpitz* reported no hits, and no damage. One Hellcat and one Seafire failed to return and one Barracuda ditched on its return from the aborted strike. The Seafires flying CAP over the Fleet shot down two Blohm und Voss flying boats as they were getting too close to the fleet. So ended 'Goodwood I'.

The Admiral kept back the battleship *Duke of York*, the carrier *Indefatigable* and seven destroyers and detached the carriers *Formidable* and *Furious*, two cruisers and the remaining destroyers to rendezvous with the fleet oil tankers and the third group, comprising *Trumpeter* and *Nabob* with their escort group of frigates, to refuel from planned resources elsewhere. Unfortunately, they were not flying A/S Swordfish and they steamed into the path of a U-boat which was probably—judging by its position—travelling from Narvik to the Atlantic. *Nabob* was torpedoed in the stern and a frigate, HMS *Bickerton*, was sunk. Eventually the carrier, which was still able to move under her own steam, was ordered back to Scapa Flow, escorted by HMS *Trumpeter*, HMCS *Algonquin* and the Fifth Escort Group. This effectively scuppered any plans for the Avengers to conduct a mining operation.

'Goodwood II', planned for 22 August, was intended to be a series of guerrilla attacks while the weather was still favourable, with the objective of persuading the Germans activate their full defensive arrangements in the (forlorn) hope that they might run out of fuel for the smoke generators before the next major strike. At 1830 *Indefatigable* launched seven Hellcats (1840 Squadron) loaded with 500-pound MC bombs and seven Fireflies (1770 Squadron). Not being hindered by the slower Barracudas, they were able to reach the coast quickly and, remaining at low level all the way, indeed reached Kaafjord before the smoke generators started. The Hellcats were able to start their bombing runs from about 8,000 feet. There were several near-misses but no hits. There were no casualties amongst the aircraft, although the Germans claimed eight aircraft shot down in the first attack and four in the second. The following day, as preparations were being made for a second guerrilla strike, the ship encountered fog and flying was cancelled.

'Goodwood III', 23 August, got under way as soon as *Formidable* and *Furious* had re-joined *Indefatigable* after refuelling but, although the weather at sea was good and the strike was launched, as the aircraft approached the coast they encountered low cloud and the leader decided to cancel the sortie and return to the fleet.

The following day the weather around the fleet was unsuitable for flying during the forenoon, but around midday it cleared so the operation was revived and the strike was launched at 1430. There were thirty-three Barracudas, all loaded with 1,600-pound AP bombs, from 820, 826, 827 and 828 Squadrons (and I was very excited to be part of one of the 827 Squadron aircrews); twenty-four Corsairs, of which five were loaded with 1,100-pound AP bombs, from 1841 and 1842 Squadrons; ten Fireflies from 1770; ten Hellcats, each carrying a 500-pound MC bomb, from 1840 Squadron; and, lastly, eight Seafires from 887 Squadron, which were to attack Banak, the airfield closest to Kaafjord.

The weather could not have been better, and we could see the Norwegian coast from about 60 miles. Needless to say, the Germans detected the strike early and, of course, the slow speed of the Barracudas allowed plenty of time for the smoke to do its job.

Below: The approach to Kaafjord by a Barracuda armed with a 1,600-pound bomb, with the German smoke generators at full pelt shrouding the target. Aircraft '4S' did not take part in 'Tungsten', so the operation under way is probably either 'Mascot' or one of the 'Goodwoods'. In the latter, both 826's and 827's Barracudas used code letters containing the numeral '4'.

Left: A photograph of HMS *Victorious* taken in 1944 and showing Corsairs amidships and Barracudas ranged aft. The four armoured fleet carriers of the *Illustrious* class (two further, modified units were joining the Navy at about this time) were very successful ships; *Victorious* herself underwent major reconstruction after the war and served until the late 1960s.

flying. Thus, with the brash confidence of youth, I just knew that I was fireproof.

The fjord was full of smoke but the heavy AA fire from *Tirpitz* gave away her position, so at least we had an aiming point. Perhaps, if the Germans had held their fire, we would have had to abandon the attack altogether. Looking back on it, what has really stuck in my mind was how completely our dive bombing training and practice at Loch Eriboll took hold. I was able to carry out a copybook attack, releasing my armour-piercing bomb at 4,000 feet to allow it to reach its terminal velocity so that, if it were to hit, it would penetrate much of the armour and seriously damage the interior of the ship instead of causing the superficial damage the lighter bombs had inflicted.

As far as my crew and I were concerned, the getaway from the attack was quite uneventful. I do not remember encountering any flak and, like Sub-Lieutenant (now Rear-Admiral) Robertson, I was delighted to see Norwegians on the balconies of their homes, sometimes quite isolated dwellings, waving Union Jacks as we flew past at low level down the fjord heading back to the sea. We landed back on *Furious* after a round trip of 2 hours 20 minutes.

Sadly, two Hellcats and one Corsair were shot down. Postwar German translations indicate that there were two hits during the attack, one by a 500-pound MC bomb which struck the light AA gun position on 'B' turret, which of course destroyed the gun position but only dented the roof of the turret itself. The second hit was by a 1,600-pound AP bomb (was it mine, perhaps?) which struck close to the bridge on the port side. This bomb did its job to the extent that it penetrated five decks having passed through a total of about six inches of armour, but it failed to explode and on examination it was found that not only had the fuse failed to function, but the bomb had less than half of the explosive which should have filled it, the rest being made up with sand. I do believe that *Tirpitz* must have been launched under a particularly lucky star.

Furious was detached to the Faeroes and my crew and one other were transferred to *Indefatigable* with two Seafires, to replace losses.

Although the weather forecasts were again pessimistic, 'Goodwood IV' was planned for the 29th and, luckily for the strike force, the weather cleared

The Hellcats and Corsairs were detached early and reached the target before the smokescreen was complete, and the Hellcats were able to deliver their bombs, seeing one hit and a number of very near misses. The Corsairs did a magnificent job in subduing the flak, and by the time the Barracudas arrived, five minutes later, there was only the heavy AA fire filling the box barrage above the target. When I first saw this, I must admit that it looked very menacing, but my observer pointed out that what I could see was the smoke from shells which had exploded: firing had been going on for some time, so what was visible was not related to the density of the barrage through which we would be sufficiently for the aircraft to be launched at 1530. The two fleet carriers launched twenty-nine Barracudas, all loaded with 1,600-pound AP bombs, two Corsairs with 1,100-pound AP bombs, three Hellcats with 500-pound MC bombs, fifteen Corsairs and ten Fireflies as escorts and flak-suppression and seven Seafires for a diversionary attack on an airfield at Hammerfest. Sadly, the bombing attacks were completely frustrated by the most effective smokescreen and all the aircraft were reduced to bombing blind. There were some near-misses, but no real damage was caused.

Although many people in the strike force envisaged further such operations, 'Goodwood' proved to be the last of the Fleet Air Arm's attempts to neutralise the German battleship. Everyone was now quite clear that the Barracuda was too slow an aircraft to be used for attacks on targets so far inland (*Tirpitz* was holed up 80 miles from the coast), allowing the enemy plenty of time to establish his smokescreen. The Corsairs and Hellcats would have been able to beat the start of the smoke generators, but none of these could carry the 1,600-pound AP and the necessary modifications would take some time. In any case, very few of their pilots had sufficient bombing training, and without accurate delivery all the efforts would probably have been in vain. These constraints on another operation meant that the summer would pass, and no one could foresee much hope of success as winter weather and early darkness were rapidly approaching. There is no doubt that the Allies had been lucky that Hitler had lost faith in his capital ships, and also that Germany was not prepared to release fighters from mainland Europe to protect *Tirpitz*.

The mighty battleship remained a potential threat to the Russian convoys in particular and to our sea communications in general, in exactly the same way as had her sister-ship *Bismarck* over three years earlier. The RAF investigated the possibility of flying Mosquitos off carriers and landing them in Russia, but the same constraints applied to these aircraft as to the Corsairs and Hellcats, and so the idea drifted off into oblivion.

* * *

For over two years, the presence of *Tirpitz* in Norwegian waters had tied up significant Allied naval forces. During that time she had been attacked not only by the Fleet Air Arm but also by the RAF. Bomber Command had launched attacks on nineteen occasions in 1940–41 and four times in 1944, utilising sixteen different types of aircraft and losing seven individual aircraft. The Navy had mounted one operation in 1942 and six in 1944. Twelve torpedo-carrying Albacores had been used and there had been 176 Barracuda launches; eleven different types of naval aircraft had been involved, and a total of six Barracudas had been lost.

Of the six separate operations carried out in 1944—'Tungsten', 'Planet', 'Brawn', 'Tiger Claw', 'Mascot' and 'Goodwood' I–IV—only 'Tungsten' had been successful, the rest being foiled either by weather or by smoke, almost certainly because the Barracuda was too slow and took too long to climb to height, giving the target defences plenty of time to be fully activated. During 'Tungsten' the Barracudas had dropped 26.25 tons of mixed types of bombs and achieved fifteen hits, which had disabled the battleship for a mere six weeks.

When, subsequently, RAF Lancasters took on the responsibility for attempting to disable or sink *Tirpitz*, they carried out three different operations, 'Paravane', 'Obviate' and 'Catechism'. Both 'Paravane' and 'Catechism' achieved success. During the former, 21 Lancasters carrying Tallboy 'M's dropped 112.5 tons of bombs and achieved one hit which disabled the target, causing the Germans to decide that it was no longer an operational asset and to use it at Tromsø as a fixed battery for local defence. Operation 'Obviate' was totally frustrated by weather, and in Operation 'Catechism' 29 Lancasters with Tallboy 'M's dropped 155.4 tons of bombs and achieved two direct hits and one near-miss, causing *Tirpitz* to capsize.

There is no doubt that *Tirpitz* was the most important target ever attacked by Barracudas, and my only thought, with hindsight, is that if a higher proportion of the aircraft on the 3 April attack had carried 1,600-pound armour-piercing bombs, then amongst the number of hits on the target there might have been one or two which could have caused much more serious damage.

While the great majority of the attacks had been using bombs, throughout the period, the squadrons had still been carrying out strikes against enemy shipping, including combined bombing and torpedo attacks. The number of targets justifying the use of torpedoes appears to have been very limited (I have been unable to establish how many sorties were flown off the Norwegian coast), and so it was no surprise when in July 1945 the Admiralty more or less abandoned the concept of airborne torpedo attacks.

From Tungsten to Minneriya *Lieutenant (A) Arthur Towlson DSC RNVR*

During the winter of 1943/44 the German battleship *Tirpitz* had undergone repair in Kaafjord. High, steep mountains on both sides made any air attack a very difficult undertaking, especially for torpedo bombers as they were unable to come down low enough to drop their missiles.

Tirpitz was not ready for sea again until after the X-craft attack (Operation 'Source') that had taken place in September 1943, but at first light on 3 April she was getting ready to leave Kaafjord to run trials in Altenfjord outside.

It was dawn on a lovely spring morning and the net gates were opening. A tug came nosing alongside . . . and then the mountain valleys echoed with the sound of scores of aircraft. Hardly had the alarm rattlers gone when bombs fell bursting all around.

There were many hits, and the ship was covered with reddish-brown clouds from bursting bombs and smoke from her own flak. Then everything stopped, the echoes died away and the fjord was still again It has taken less than a minute, but *Tirpitz* had been terribly damaged.

There had been fifteen hits by bombs 500-pounders and 1,600-pounders. Some had penetrated the upper armoured deck and, bursting below, had done great damage. None, however, had penetrated the lower 8-inch armoured deck, so the ship was still afloat, although some 120 men had been killed and 316 wounded, including the Captain. It was quickly followed by a second attack, but by then the effect of surprise had worn off and less was achieved.

The two strikes had been launched from the aircraft carriers *Victorious*, *Furious*, *Searcher*, *Fencer*, *Emperor* and *Pursuer*, the first strike of twenty-one Barracuda dive bombers and the second twenty Barracudas, each with fighter escort. The attack was timed to coincide with the running of another convoy to Russia which included the battleship *Royal Sovereign*.

The German administration had failed to heed its staff recommendations about improved AA defences. In just two minutes, the Fleet Air Arm had ruined much of the six months of repair work and had inflicted incalculable harm upon the morale of the ship's company as it was about to recover after the X-craft attack. Although no damage was done to the warship's main or auxiliary machinery, the near-misses had caused flooding, the W/T aerials were again wrecked, the upper deck was a shambles, with damage to the AA armament, and the casualty list was formidable.

It had been a sad day for 829 Squadron, flying from *Victorious*, having lost Sub-Lieutenants Bowles and Whittaker and Leading Airman Colwell on take-off, probably because they turned too quickly in order to clear their slipstream from the next Barracuda to take off, and Sub-Lieutenants Richardson and Cannon and Leading Airman Carroll to anti-aircraft gun fire over the target. Bill Ryan, Bill Firth and I, in Barracuda '4R', approached *Tirpitz* in position with the Squadron, but smoke was already partially covering the target, requiring me to miss dropping my single 1,600-pound bomb along the fore-and-aft line of the ship and to continue my approach until a better view of her was possible. Thus my drop was delayed for a little, until we were on the beam. I remember a clear view of a boat hurriedly leaving the battleship's side.

On our return to Scapa Flow we were honoured by a visit by HM King George VI, who made inspections of crew and aircrews and dined in the wardroom. The ship was also

Opposite page: 'Tungsten' strike force. These thirteen aircraft are doubtless part of the first wave (827 and 830 Squadrons), since five Barracudas can be seen to be armed with single 1,600-pound bombs; for the second strike (829 and 831), only two aircraft were so armed. The majority of the remaining Barracudas were each armed with three 500-pound SAP or MC; since they are not carrying anything beneath the fuselage, they are thus flying with an asymmetric underwing load—there was no difficulty trimming out a Barracuda's rudder the 'normalise' this.

Right: The writer as a sub-lieutenant in the cockpit of the Barracuda (thought to be '4A') normally flown by Sub-Lieutenant Stuart Taylor RNZVR, which displays the emblem 'Hells Bells' and features a mission symbol denoting his success in hitting the target in the 'Tungsten' strike.

visited, and the crews inspected, by General Bernard Montgomery, who must have been delighted that his invasion forces would not suffer *Tirpitz*'s presence on D-Day!

On 26 April, in Operation 'Ridge Able', Barracudas of 829 and 831 Squadrons in company with *Victorious*'s Corsair fighters were tasked with intercepting and destroying any German located shipping in the 'leads' between the Lofoten Islands and mainland Norway. A merchant ship escorted by three flak vessels was sighted and first attacked by the Corsairs with their 0.5-inch machine guns to get heads down and then bombed by the Barracudas. The attack was successful, and it could be seen that all ships were in distress and that the merchantman was on fire, and it was not necessary to drop more bombs. Staying at height and the presence of a snowstorm led to contact with other aircraft being lost, and our orders were that if no shipping was intercepted we were to continue to Bodø, the German convoy assembly point and bomb ships there. It was considered that a number of damaged ships was a better outcome than one sunk as this would prove more of a difficulty to the enemy since German docks would become congested.

Approaching Bodø in a snowstorm was difficult and, for once, remaining above the cloud seemed a better option in spite of the difficulty of descending over mountainous terrain. However, after experiencing anti-aircraft shelling, which more or less gave away the position of the port, we were lucky enough to spot a clear 'chimney' through the clouds and could see that we were over water, so down we went, circling through the chimney but picking up speed all the time. On clearing the base of the clouds we discovered that we were over Bodø harbour, where several ships were moored and alongside docks. Our speed now was far too fast to make any sort of an accurate dive to bomb, so it was necessary to lose speed by flying upwards, carry out a stall turn and then to make an aiming dive on to one of the ships in the harbour, a vessel of some 6,000 tons, before continuing our dive to sea level and making our escape to seaward and on to *Victorious* some 100 miles distant. The return was at low level in order to make ourselves as invisible as possible, and we noticed what appeared to be a large enemy aircraft in the distance that was probably hoping to find and shadow any Allied ships. On landing back on board we discovered that our Barracuda, '4R', had been hit by shrapnel, causing holes in the rudder and elevators.

My next offensive sortie in '4R' was on 1 June as part of Operation 'Lombard', when 829 Squadron's Barracudas and Corsairs intercepted three enemy merchant vessels accompanied by five flak ships in the 'leads' south of Ålesund. We attacked the largest merchant vessel in the centre of the convoy, and hits were observed. In total two MVs were sunk and one MV and all three flak ships left burning.

* * *

In June 1944, on passage through the Mediterranean en route to the Far East, 829 Squadron were flying twelve Barracudas with full crews on an exercise, dive bombing a raft towed by *Victorious*. Alarmingly, the wings of two Barracudas folded and both aircraft crashed into the sea, killing all six crew members. I recall that Lieutenant (A) Grindrod RNVR, Sub-Lieutenant (A) P. Hollis RNVR and Leading Airman I. Kitley were among them. My recollection is that the locking pins of the folding wings were suspect, being made of mild steel in lieu of high-tensile steel.

This incident affected the morale of some of the newer members of the Squadron, and Lieutenant-Commanders Rance and Phillips, the Wing and Squadron Commanding Officers, respectively, requested that I give them as much confidence in the Barracudas as I could. This, I believe, was helped when I looped my aircraft over the runway at Minneriya, Ceylon, keeping the wings firmly attached in the process.

For dive-bombing operations over Sumatra, air–sea rescue facilities were provided by a submarine which would lie offshore. Aircraft not able to return to *Victorious* some 100 miles away could ditch alongside the submarine for the crew to be picked up. The crews of any Barracuda forced to land or crash inland were to make their way to a named isolated beach to which the submarine would return some four days later. In order to prove to the Captain of the submarine on the conning tower who you were and that there was no Japanese ambush, we were informed that we should stand with our backs to the submarine, lower our trousers to the ankles, bend over and look towards our rescuers between our legs!

TO BECCLES AND BEYOND

Lieutenant-Commander Robert McCandless DSC

WHILE the Home Fleet, on Prime Minister Churchill's instructions, was committed to trying to disable or sink *Tirpitz* as well as protecting the Murmansk convoys against U-boats and preventing enemy shipping from moving along the Norwegian coast (an almost impossible task in the prevailing weather conditions), the Eastern Fleet was not idle.

In the early part of 1944, the only fleet carrier available for the Eastern Fleet was HMS *Illustrious*. In the tropical and sub-tropical conditions in that theatre, the Barracudas needed the entire length of the fleet carriers' flight decks for take-off because the hot air reduced the power of the engine.

810 and 847 Squadrons were allocated to *Illustrious*, which, on 19 April, in concert with the American aircraft carrier *Saratoga*, launched a strike on Sabang (Sumatra). Eighteen Barracudas took part, eight from 847 and ten from 810. Each aircraft was armed with two 500-pound MC and two 250-pound GP bombs. The Barracudas followed the American strike force—no doubt because they were slower—and at 10,500 feet they were able to fly unopposed to their targets. As a result of the attack, fires were started in the harbour installations and at the nearby airfield, where many aircraft were destroyed. Two merchant vessels were set ablaze and the power station destroyed, and oil storage tanks were set on fire. No aircraft were lost. On 17 May the raid was repeated at Soerabaya (Java) and an oil refinery was destroyed.

Before the next strike, the Barracudas were stripped of everything that could be removed without reducing the efficiency of the aircraft as dive bombers. It was hoped that this would perhaps increase the speed of the aircraft and its rate of climb. Then, on 21 June, thirteen Barracudas and thirty-five Corsairs attacked Port Blair in the Andaman Islands, where considerable damage was inflicted upon harbour installations, while a power station and a radar station were destroyed. One Barracuda was shot down.

On 25 July a second strike was carried out against Sabang, after which *Illustrious* went to Durban for refit and was replaced by *Victorious* with 822 Squadron on board and *Indomitable* with 815 and 817. On 24 August these three squadrons carried out a combined strike with 32 aircraft against a large cement works at Indaroeng and harbour installations at Emmahaven (Sumatra), causing moderate damage at both. No aircraft were lost.

On 18 September there was another joint strike by eighteen aircraft against the important rail centre at Sigli on Sumatra, where considerable damage was caused to repair sheds and the complex rail network. After this raid *Indomitable* and her two squadrons detached from *Victorious* and on 17 and 19 October bombed Japanese defences on the Nicobar Islands. Twenty aircraft were involved and one was shot down. These were the last carrier-borne strikes undertaken by Fairey Barracudas.

The only contribution made by Barracudas in the Mediterranean Fleet was during the Salerno landings in 1943, when they carried out A/S patrols while the flight decks were required by fighters protecting the ships which were closer inshore.

* * *

After Operation 'Goodwood', 827 Squadron returned to Hatston, and I was surprised to find that we were still carrying out trials with the 'B' bomb—and still we were being given no information about the time taken for the bomb to sink and return to the surface. Little wonder, then, that there was very little enthusiasm on our part for this trial. I carried out four more sorties but I have no idea how many were conducted out by the Squadron in total. The trials just ceased, without comment from anyone.

It was now some time since the Squadron had had any practice for torpedo dropping, so amongst other exercises we carried out some ALTs in combination with 830 Squadron. As always with these mass attacks, I felt that the scope for collisions was very great, but I never heard of any, nor even of near-misses.

I was sent off on some errand, with only my TAG for company, from Hatston to RNAS Donibristle, a fairly small airfield just east of Rosyth at the northern end of the Forth railway bridge. We called in at East Haven on the way south, then at Donibristle we did whatever it was we were sent to do and set off back to Hatston. The weather was absolutely foul,

Above: While 827 Squadron were engaged in Operation 'Goodwood', Barracudas were also delivering ordnance against enemy installations on the other side of the world. Here aircraft of 817 Squadron (HMS *Indomitable*) are on their way to strike at Japanese targets in the East Indies.

with about a 200 foot cloud base, rain and poor visibility. I was too inexperienced to say that I was not going to return to base in such awful weather, and so we took off. At this time air-to-ground radio was fairly limited in range and reliability and there were no radio aids for descent through cloud, so I flew over the sea, hugging the coast on my port side and with a fairly clear idea of where I was all the time and knowing what to expect next. When we reached Burghead on the Moray Firth, I decided that I was not going to risk flying straight across and turned west, carrying on until I reached RAF Lossiemouth. There I landed, and refuelled and took off again, still following close to the coast to Inverness then north-eastwards along the coast of Ross and Cromarty towards Thurso. When we reached Thurso I had to take my courage in both hands and set off towards the Orkneys. By now I knew the area fairly well, so I thought I would recognise my landfall immediately and I was fairly sure that there was no particularly high ground. How I managed it I don't know, but I first recognised where I was when I found myself over the Fleet anchorage in Scapa Flow. I knew that the ships had permission to fire at anything that flew over the Fleet, but I can only assume that the weather was so bad that all the guns' crews had been stood down. Just as frightening, however, was the fact that the ships' balloon barrage was still airborne. So I said to my TAG, Leading Airman Ron Hibbs, 'Ron, every balloon has to be anchored to a vessel of some kind, so if I fly past anything I see at low level, then we ought to miss the cables!' That is what I did, and I found Hatston and landed. I never mentioned this to anyone, and no one seemed surprised that I had come back in such awful weather: perhaps it was considered to be normal routine and unworthy of comment. At least Ron was grateful for a safe return: he told me so some fifty-five years later!

BARRACUDA

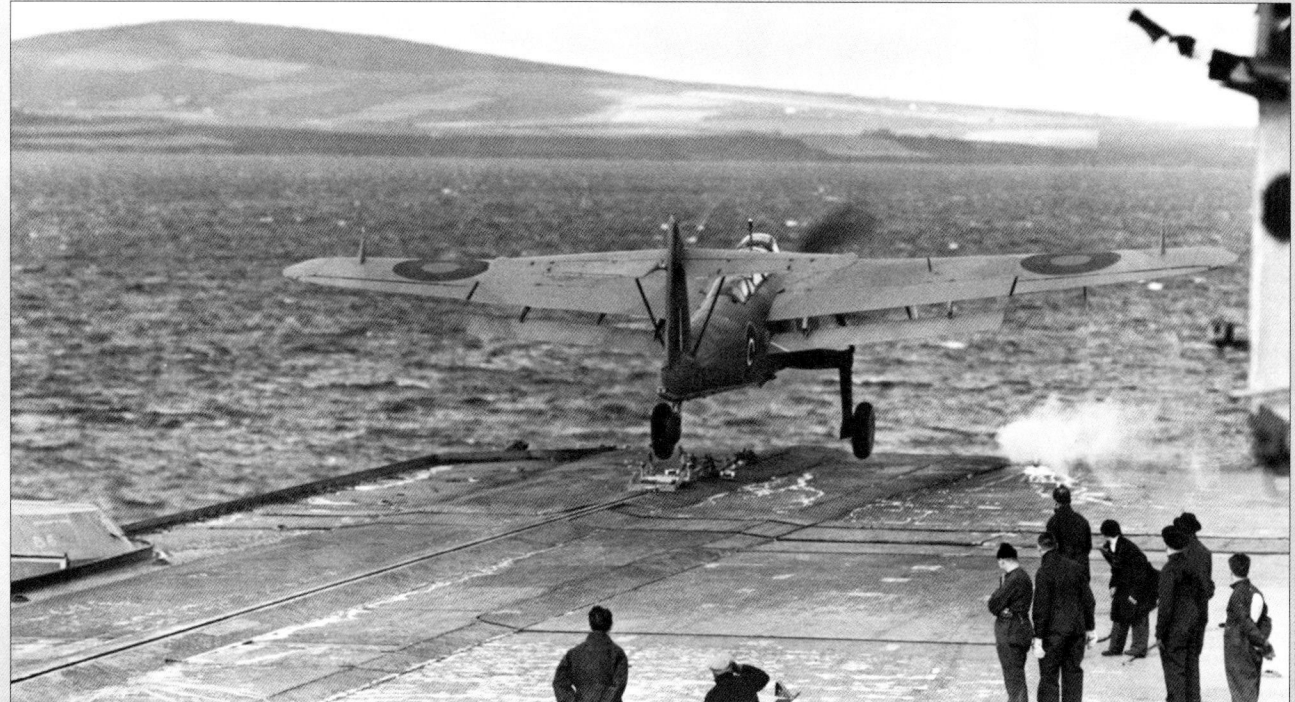

Shortly after that episode, the Squadron was sent to join Coastal Command at RAF Beccles in Suffolk. Our job was to patrol the Dutch and German coastline at night to try to stop any shipping moving in either direction. Our aircraft were still fitted with ASV (Air to Surface Vessel) radar and it was assumed, I suppose, that this would help us in our search. The sets worked quite well and would have been useful had the seas always been as calm as a millpond, but they seldom were. If there were waves of any height at all, the radar was reflected off them, giving 'snow' all over the screen and obliterating any other reflection off a ship, if one was there. Most of the time was spent conducting 'eyeball searches', looking for a wake or, in the case of E-boats, for wakes of high-speed launches.

If our navigation was a bit out and we got too close to the coast, for example at Den Helder, the display of anti-aircraft fire was most impressive. Needless to say, on such occasions discretion became the better part of valour and we continued our fruitless task in the Stygian darkness.

Once when I had been on the first of the night's searches and I had returned, with nothing to report, and had repaired to bed, I was somewhat rudely awakened in the early hours by one of the stewards who told me that someone had found some ships and bombed one of them and that we were all required to go out again. I was told that Group Captain Clouston's remark was 'Fill them up with rum and send them out again!' So we had two full English breakfasts that night.

One of the hazards involved in flying from Beccles out to the North Sea was that the airfield was close to the 'Divers Gun Belt'. This was a narrow strip along the Essex and Suffolk coastline which was heavily armed with AA guns of various sizes. The gunners had been ordered to fire at anything flying in from seaward, including V-1s of course, without attempting to find out whether it was friend or foe. And they did. Thus if our navigation was a bit awry because of inaccurate wind forecasts, it would be a very nasty welcome home. For this reason we were moved lock, stock and barrel to RAF Langham in Norfolk at the end of October, where we stayed until 14 December, when again we were moved, this time to RNAS Machrihanish on the Mull of Kintyre.

We found out that we were there awaiting the arrival of the first of the new light fleet carriers, HMS *Colossus*, which was to take us to join the British Pacific Fleet. With a number of new crews having joined the Squadron, we began polishing up our carrier drill, torpedo attacks and ADDLs. We even had the opportunity to do some practice deck landings on HMS *Patroller*, one of the American-built escort carriers.

The New Year 1945 was ' brought in' in some style. We carried out two squadron runner torpedo attacks on a ship in the Firth of Clyde, quite close to Ailsa Craig, which seemed to go quite well, but I don't remember if we were ever told how many hits we scored, or indeed whether we had hit anything at all. Anyway, it gave us cause for thought about the future.

A fortnight later we embarked in *Colossus*. The next ten days were spent carrying out exercises for the benefit of the ship as well as for sharpening up our own performance. It was at this time that I experienced my first accelerated take-off. The Barracuda was taxied on to the after end of the 'catapult' and a fairly sizeable cradle was moved back under the aircraft, whereupon two ratings on each side guided a hinged leg from the cradle on to four strongpoints on its lower fuselage. As the cradle moved slowly forward, the hinged legs lifted the after end of the fuselage up until the aircraft was in its flying attitude. The ratings cleared out of the way as soon as it was confirmed that the cradle legs were properly positioned. The Flight Deck Officer (FDO) stood where the pilot and the launch operator could see him clearly. He carried two flags, one red and one green. On the far side of the deck from him stood the Flight Deck Engineer Officer (FDEO), whose job it was to confirm that the aircraft had been properly loaded. He also had two flags. When he showed his green flag, the FDO raised his own green flag above his head and waved it to indicate to the pilot that he should pull the booster override and to open his throttle to take-off power. When the pilot was satisfied that all was well and that he had tightened the throttle to hold it in the fully open position, he would raise his hand to the FDO, place his left hand on the throttle quadrant behind the throttle to make sure that it would not close due to the 'g' imposed by

Left, top: A Barracuda about to be launched from the booster—sometimes referred to, rather imprecisely, as a catapult—on board HMS *Colossus* in the Clyde, January 1945. The cradle holds the aircraft in the flying attitude and the FDEO's flag is raised while the FDO signals the launch.
Left, centre: The aircraft departs, leaving the collapsed cradle behind at the forward end of the booster track; the ship here is one of the armoured fleet carriers. This was not a particularly speedy method of flying off aircraft, but in the event of, say, an obstructed flight deck, it was a valuable option.
Left, bottom: Another accelerator-boosted departure, this time from HMS *Indefatigable*, the subject being Barracuda 'K' of either 820 or 826 Squadron, summer 1944; a Seafire III looks on. Notice the 'C' Type roundels on the Barracuda's wings, and also the twin-track booster (as opposed to the single-track booster fitted to the earlier armoured carriers).

Above: Another departure via the accelerator. This early months of 1945 were a period of intensive training for the Barracuda squadrons about to embark on the light fleet carriers for service in the Far East, and booster practice was particularly invaluable given the aircraft's propensity to under-perform in hot climates.

the acceleration, his right hand would hold the control column in the mid position and he would stick his right elbow into his stomach to prevent the column from moving backwards under the same 'g' force. Lastly, he would press his head back against the headrest to prevent 'whiplash'.

The FDO then checked with the Flying Control on the island to make sure that the green light was still on. He would contemplate the movement of the ship, watching the rise and fall of the bow under the influence of the waves, and then, at the lowest point, he would drop his green flag and the launcher would send the aircraft on its way—ideally on the 'up' stroke of the next wave. Finding that you were still in charge of the aircraft was a pleasant little surprise. The artificial horizon and the directional gyro in the instrument panel both toppled and took a minute or so to re-erect.

A week or so later, half the Squadron went ashore while the ship's Corsair squadron (1846) embarked. This they did without incident, and when they were all stowed in the hangar we in the Barracuda squadron left on board set about giving the ship and the flight deck party, and ourselves, some experience of carrier night operations. Seemingly, it was considered by Their Lordships that the Barracudas in the four light fleet carriers, *Colossus*, *Vengeance*, *Venerable* and *Glory*, would be used mainly for night bombing attacks after we joined the BPF, so we should start to practise now. This experience was to be given, first, by a flight of four Barracudas, of which I was one. The drill was to be a free take-off followed by a circuit of the ship, and then, at intervals of a few minutes, we would land-on in sequence, catch a wire, be pushed back to the take-off point and go off again. We were briefed that the brilliance of the lighting would be reduced progressively during the exercise to see how well we coped.

I was last of the four to take off, and I found the task perfectly straightforward. The radio chat between each of the flight in turn with the ship let

Left: Barracudas and Corsairs pack the flight deck of HMS *Colossus* on passage to Malta and en route to join the British Pacific Fleet, 12 March 1945.

me know when it was my turn to join the circuit. The lighting on the ship was bright, I was able to pick out the batsman's signals clearly and my first landing was entirely satisfactory. Off again, and we were told that the brilliance would be reduced to half. Again, all was clear and went well. The last of our three landings was, to put it mildly, something of a surprise. With the exception of the ship's navigation lights, the blue outline lights and the batsman's lights, all others would be extinguished. The blue lights could not be seen from the circuit and I was hoping that I would be able to see when to turn-in on to finals. To be honest, I hadn't realised until then just how clearly the luminescence of the wake would show, and in the event the circuit was as easy to judge as it had been in daylight. So the three landings went well for us, to the satisfaction of all concerned.

Exercises of all kinds continued throughout February, then, after a short stay alongside for storing, the ship set off for the Mediterranean with *Vengeance* (flying the flag of the Admiral) and *Venerable*. We were carrying so many spare aircraft to be disembarked to Malta that we were unable to fly at all during this passage. We flew off the spares and returned to the ship by boat, following which we set off independently for Egypt, disembarking to RNAS Dekheila.

During our six weeks ashore in Dekheila, VE-Day was celebrated at a stadium in Alexandria and all the services provided about 1,000 men to take part in the parade. Each service formed up in separate blocks and, presumably because I was the noisiest, I was appointed commander of the front platoon of the naval contingent. A Royal Marine band was playing military music, and I think most of us were feeling a bit dozy in the heat of the midday sun when I noticed a bit of movement around what I took to be the royal box. Then some dignitary entered. I didn't know who it was, but it occurred to me that the music was probably the National Anthem and our whole parade was still standing 'At ease'. I remarked to the Parade Commander, who was standing ahead of me, that I thought that this was the National Anthem, so we all came to 'Attention' and 'Present Arms'. Not the greatest compliment to the dignitary.

A few days later we all embarked once more to find that an Admiralty Order had told us to stop practising torpedo attacks and concentrate on dive bombing for future operations. I was detailed to lead a flight of six aircraft on a dive-bombing exercise using a target towed by the ship. After the attack, my TAG dropped a flame float a couple of miles on the beam of the ship and I started to orbit around it so

Below: The ships of Aircraft Carrier Group 11, i.e. HM Ships *Colossus*, *Vengeance*, *Venerable* and *Glory*—all four together for the first and last time, at Alexandria, 26 May 1945. The sixteen light fleet carriers of the *Colossus/Majestic* class were remarkable vessels. After the war many were updated and sold for service in foreign navies: *Vengeance*, for example, served in the Royal Australian and the Brazilian Navies, and was not finally scrapped until 2004.

Left: VE-Day celebrations at Alexandria, May 1945: the Services contingents march past.
Below: Damage to Barracuda PM826/'B', back on dry ground after it had been struck in a mid-air collision over Egypt in May 1945. Skilful flying by the author assured the safety of his crew, but two other aircraft involved in the incident were less fortunate.
Right: The four vessels of the 11th ACG arrived in the waters off the sub-continent more or less at the same time. *Colossus* embarked the 14th Carrier Air Group (827 Squadron's Barracudas and 1846 Squadron's Corsairs), *Glory* the 16th CAG (837 and 1832 Squadrons, similarly equipped), *Vengeance* the 13th CAG (812 and 1850 Squadrons, the same) and *Venerable* (seen here) the 15th CAG (814 and 1851 Squadrons, the same). None saw action.

that the division could re-form ready for us to land-on. When I looked out to my starboard side, the aircraft which had joined me there should have been line astern, so I signalled to him to go back, then I looked over my left shoulder to see where the others were. Suddenly, I was no longer in charge of the aircraft. With the usual speed associated with the urgent need to survive, I got control again and said to my observer, 'What the —— was that?' He said that one of the other aircraft had hit us and that two aircraft had crashed. Since we were flying at about 2,000 feet I knew that the crews would have no chance of survival.

The observer then said that there was a huge hole in the trailing edge of our starboard wing, the outboard hinge of the Youngman flap had gone and the flap was being held on only by the inboard hinge.

The flap itself was banging on the fuselage, and then he said, 'It's gone.' I found the ailerons very stiff to move, and it became even more obvious that I was not going to be landing back on the ship. I called up and told them I was going back ashore to Dekheila. Bearing in mind the asymmetric damage to the aircraft, I knew that I had no way of estimating how, or at what speed, a stall would occur, so I told the crew that I would be landing at the same speed as I was flying then and warned Air Traffic at the airfield as well. The touch-down, with my tail high in the air, must have looked distinctly odd, but at least it was safe, and we stopped before the end of the runway. When I got out of the aircraft and looked at the damage, I was horrified to see that the tail fin of the other aircraft had driven a hole into the trailing edge as deep as the main spar. However, we had been lucky in two particular ways. First, the outboard end of the hole stopped at the point where, although the aileron was damaged, it was still moving on two hinges, and, secondly, the point where the hole stopped against the main spar was just where the aluminium-tube aileron controls were dented but not bent (hence the stiffness). Yet another of my nine lives gone.

We carried on with more exercises until 28 May, when *Colossus* and *Vengeance* navigated the Suez Canal and proceeded down the Red Sea. It was shortly after this that we continued with night flying and now, for the first time for all of us, we were to be boosted off. It will be recalled that, during a Barracuda's accelerated take-off, the artificial horizon and directional gyro both toppled, leaving us dependent on the turn-and-bank indicator and the climb-and-descent instrument to help us keep straight and climbing gently with the wings level. Well, of course, at night, the need for flying instruments is paramount, so there is no doubt that one tends to be somewhat tense. However, the kind sailors in the escorting destroyer took up a position two cables ahead of the carrier when it was into wind for flying and they showed three lights at their masthead, so, for the first few seconds after take-off, there was an external reference which most certainly did help. Sadly, one aircraft failed to return from the exercise and it had to be assumed that he flew into the sea after take-off because there had been absolutely no radio contact.

After a search of the area, we carried on down the Red Sea and stopped briefly at Aden before continuing along the west coast of India, in monsoon weather for the best part of a week before the Barracudas were disembarked to RNAS Katukurunda (HMS *Ukussa*—Sinhalese for 'hawk') and the Corsairs went to RAF Tambaram near Madras. Our aircraft were modified for Rocket-Assisted Take-Off Gear and we all experienced such a departure at least once. RATOG was a kit of two light pieces of metal framework (one for each side) which attached to the two forward strongpoints on to which the boosting cradle fitted. The framework supported either one or two rockets each side and the rockets were fired by pressing a button on top of the throttle lever. We were briefed that the angle at which these rockets were held on the strongpoints ensured that the thrust was aimed at the centre of gravity of the aircraft. Therefore, if one side failed to fire, the aircraft would still remain straight on take-off and not be forced off to one side or the other. I suppose this was checked by test pilots, but I was wary and did not press the button until I was already passing the island.

Early in July 1945 we re-embarked in *Colossus*, collected the Corsairs from Madras and sailed in company with *Vengeance* and the destroyers *Tyrian* and *Tuscan*. We used RATOG on our first take-off and all went well, but to be honest, none of us really noticed any marked difference. It was at about this time that we were told that the policy in the BPF was to fly our Barracudas as two-seater aircraft (or even as single-seaters), so seven of our observers were appointed away from the squadron and it was intended that we would fly with TAGS only.

Above: A BPF-marked Barracuda departs with the assistance of RATOG; the aircraft is not loaded and has lifted off quite easily. The ship is again HMS *Colossus*: her deck letter here is 'C', but this would quickly be changed to 'D'.

Below: 814 Squadron Barracudas at Katukurunda, June 1945. The aircraft at far left still sports European-style markings, while others have Eastern Fleet *décor*. BPF markings would soon replace both (see page 120).

We continued to fly off small numbers just to keep everyone in practice while we were on passage to Fremantle in Western Australia. We were there for less than twenty-four hours before setting off again, round the southern coast of Australia, until, as we were approaching Sydney, we were disembarked to Jervis Bay, a small airfield some seventy miles or so to the south of the city. Jervis Bay—HMS *Nabswick*—had no service accommodation, so we found ourselves billeted in a hotel, which was very comfortable. Meanwhile the ship went into dock in Sydney to have her 20mm Oerlikon AA guns exchanged for 40mm Bofors.

During this period we were granted seven days' leave and many of us elected to spend the time in Sydney, using *Colossus* as a B&B. There were two things which surprised us. First, the enormous steak breakfasts, which seemed to be fairly standard, and secondly, the very early closing time for the pubs (6 p.m., if I remember correctly), so there was something of a break until the night clubs started to open. But we coped!

On our return from leave, there did not appear to be much flying planned and the aircraft were being stripped of a lot of equipment to reduce their weight and improve their performance in the hot weather. The observers' blister windows were removed and replaced with Perspex flush with the fuselage. The ASV set and aerials were removed, together with the HF set, the TAG's machine guns, ammunition and seat and much else. We re-embarked on 13 August and the ship returned to Sydney the following day.

At 0900 on 13 August 1945, Mr Attlee, the new Prime Minister, announced that the war was over, following the dropping of the atomic bomb over Japan a couple of days earlier. Seven TAGs left the ship in a hurry, including my own, Leading Airman Ron Hibbs, and I didn't get the chance to say goodbye. I was sad about that: we had been through some interesting times together.

We sailed that afternoon, leaving a wildly excited and jubilant Sydney, and we were told that we would be sailing up the coast of China, to Shanghai in particular, to enforce the peace if necessary and to start recovering our prisoners-of-war from that area. We had embarked doctors, nurses and POW liaison officers. There was a delay before we went on to Shanghai in order to give the Japanese the opportunity to get the message across to all their outposts that the war was, in fact, over and that they were not to resist the occupying forces. During this time we did very little flying—just enough to keep ourselves and the ships in practice—and we spent a lot of time at anchor off various American-controlled islands. No leave was granted, and it was all very tedious.

In early September the ship was sent to Formosa (Taiwan) to fly some of our doctors and nurses ashore. The Americans had rescued all the POWs able to walk, but over a hundred wounded had had to stay ashore and required attention. The Americans had left medical and other supplies.

More POW liaison teams were transferred from cruisers for air passage to Shanghai. Nine Barracudas were used to fly them ashore to Kiang Wan, where the CO had a mishap on landing and damaged his aircraft. He had decided not to land on the main runway in case it had been sabotaged, and all nine aircraft landed on a straight stretch of taxi strip! Incidentally, ATC was still Japanese, but of course there was no communication—we simply landed. While we were there, the Japanese offered each of us a tiny cup of green tea, which we accepted, although not many of us actually drank it. During our little tea ceremony a white, twin-engined aircraft taxied out and took off. Our Corsairs were overhead, so we watched to see what would happen. When the aircraft reached an altitude of a couple of hundred feet, it rolled over and promptly dived into the ground. None of the Japanese moved; they merely stared. The interpreter asked what had happened and he was told that the aircraft had a group of senior officers on board who were ashamed of having to surrender their arms: this was their way of committing *hara-kiri*. We returned to *Colossus* and collected further liaison teams, flying them ashore to the same place, and then the ship sailed for Korea to pick up about 600 POWs who were capable of walking.

Later that month I was detailed to carry out an air test. This was my first opportunity to find out how differently the Barracuda behaved after it had been stripped of all excess weight and had its ASV aerials and blister windows removed. Once I had satisfied myself that the aircraft was fully serviceable, I decided to try some aerobatics. Barrel rolls and slow rolls went quite well, so I thought I'd have a go at a loop. I climbed up to a fair height and went into a steep dive to gain speed, pulled back into the start of a loop and stalled out into a spin. The recovery was very straightforward, but I decided that that was enough for today! On returning to the ship, I heard that the escorting destroyer had signalled to the carrier, 'Is the Barracuda on my starboard beam all right?' The carrier had replied, 'It is his twenty-first birthday!' That was my last flying for nearly a month because the ship was dispatched to Hong Kong, where a number of our aircraft were flown ashore to Kai Tak (Kowloon). By this time the ship had been at sea—or, at least, not alongside—for sixty-three days.

The squadron officers and ratings were divided into two groups. The first group went to act as guards on the Japanese POW camp and the second,

Opposite page: Barracuda wreck recovery Ceylonese style.
Above: 827 Squadron Barracudas on exercise. *Colossus* and her air group arrived too late to see action in the Pacific War, but in the second half of August 1945 the ship was dispatched to the East China Sea to assist in 'mopping-up' operations. Meanwhile the squadrons kept their hand in—just in case trouble began to brew. Notice the VHF whip aerial alongside the main aerial post of the nearest aircraft—and also that no radar is carried.

of which I was a member, went to act as guards on the Kowloon dockyard. With a small group of ratings, I was detailed to take charge of one of the gates into the dockyard. We were required to count the coolies passing in and out of this gate and to search them thoroughly on the way out. Within two days, every rating was required to attend sick bay with infected sores on their hands, arms and bare knees. The doctor said that these sores were all caused by touching the clothing of the coolies during the searching, so needless to say, the searches became somewhat less thorough. We had an interpreter attached to our group, and he was absolutely essential. At the gate was a guardroom where those not on duty outside could relax.

Soon after we took up our duties, a group of tiny children took to congregating, staying all day and until quite late in the evening. We used to have sandwiches and tea for snacks during our twelve-hour shift and, usually, the ratings gave some of the food to the children, who wolfed it down. A girl who seemed to control the rest asked our interpreter if the children would be allowed to keep the guardroom clean in return for food, and, of course, we agreed. They made a delightful little task force who did a very good job of keeping us clean and tidy even though their ages appeared to be between six and eight. I asked the interpreter to find out the age of the leader and he said he thought she was about fourteen, explaining that they were all so tiny because of the lack of food throughout the Japanese occupation. Needless to say, the ratings scrounged even more food for our 'snacks' and doubtless the children ate what they could and took the rest home.

Opposite our gate, on the other side of the road, was an empty, five-storey block of flats. One evening, we had a telephone call from the POW camp to report that someone was signalling from this block, into the camp, and that we were to go and arrest whoever it was. It so happened that we had an outflow of coolies at the time and we could only spare one rating to come with me to search the place. Never having undertaken such a task before, and having no idea who, how many or what we might find, I was somewhat apprehensive; I'd rather have been boosted off at night in a Barracuda. I decided to leave the rating, with his rifle and fixed bayonet, on the central landing to prevent anyone moving into rooms I had already searched. I then searched every room on every floor.

It is very difficult to point a torch into every corner of a room and behind the door all at the same time, and I was beginning to work up quite a sweat. On the top floor, I found one man. Luckily, he was as frightened as I was, so we marched him off to the local police station and left him to the tender mercies of the constabulary. I have, since that experience, felt a lot of sympathy for Army personnel when they have to carry out house-to-house searches. These days, perhaps, training and better equipment help.

Towards the end of October we were re-embarked and set off towards Ceylon again, this time aiming to maintain a fairly high speed passage as the ship was required back in the Pacific to continue with the POW repatriation. The Squadron disembarked to Katukurunda, and over the next week I was required to undergo an instrument flying course in an Airspeed Oxford (twin-engined!) aircraft. I seemed to get through it to the satisfaction of the instructors because I have a large stamped assessment in my log book. We continued flying, but without a lot of enthusiasm because most of us were awaiting demobilisation. What I found somewhat difficult to understand was that amongst the exercises we carried out were practice torpedo attacks. This was distinctly odd.

Officers and ratings were all given leave during the early part of December 1945 and I, along with five of my particular chums, borrowed a small 'people carrier' vehicle from the transport department and went off on a tour of Ceylon. However, it was a somewhat shortened version of a tour and took in only Hambantota at the southern end of the island to see the enormous number of crocodiles. It was very hot and sticky. Then we went up into the mountains (6,000 feet) to Kandy to see the Temple of the Tooth (and, for me, to have a look at local methods of brewing beer), and after that, it was off to Nuwara Eliya and then Diyatalawa to a services rest camp. The weather at this altitude was absolutely marvellous—warm sunny days, and cool nights when sleep came easily and restfully, and the delightful company of some of the WAAF personnel who also used the rest camp.

On 30 December those of us who were left on the Squadron (many already having departed to return home) re-embarked in *Colossus*. We set off for Cape Town, South Africa, where the ship was to undergo a refit. We would be ashore at Wingfield. We called in at Mombasa and Durban in passing, and in Durban we threw a cocktail party on the flight deck. The after end of the flight deck had all the tables laid out with snacks and drinks; the aircraft were ranged at the forward end, leaving the midships area clear. The

Left: Three Corsairs and a Barracuda from HMS *Colossus* in close formation; the embarked Corsair squadron was 1846. In contrast to the Barracudas, which retained the Temperate Sea Scheme (Dark Sea Grey and Dark Slate Grey upper surfaces in disruptive camouflage, with Sky under surfaces) of earlier years, the Corsairs are finished in Glossy Sea Blue overall. The national markings for both types of aircraft, in keeping with the general practice for aircraft serving with the BPF, ape the US style and are devoid of any red colouring.

Right: From January to March 1946, en route home from the Far East, *Colossus* docked at Simonstown in the Union of South Africa in order to undergo a refit. The air component was shore-based at Wingfield, from where exercises and training continued. A good many photographs of 827 Squadron Barracudas exist from this period, many taken with the spectacular Cape scenery as a backdrop. This is one of them. The author's mount is '374'.

guests were brought up on to the flight deck using the aircraft lift, and they were all suitably impressed. The party went well until just before sunset, when the Royal Marine Guard and Band arrived on the flight deck to Beat Retreat and play the Evening Hymn during the Sunset Ceremony. Naturally, all the guests were watching the ceremony, and during the playing of the Evening Hymn there were tears for many of the emigrant patriots. When it was over and the Royal Marines had marched off, the guests turned round to find that all the tables, drinks and food had gone. As a result, those with whom we had been particularly friendly said, 'Oh well, you'd better come ashore with us,' and so a very pleasant evening was had by all. Next day we left Durban, the Lady in White standing on the end of the harbour wall and singing a farewell song. She must have had a powerful voice because those of us on that side of the ship could hear her quite clearly.

At Wingfield we found that our air group of Barracudas and Corsairs, together with a few Seafires, were the only flying inhabitants. We continued to fly, carrying out our usual series of navexes and dive bombing, and lots of low flying. The battleship *King George V* entered harbour for a refit and we mustered a combined strike force to welcome her and perform a fly past.

During February 1946 a Seafire flew to Port Elizabeth, 200 or so miles to the east of Cape Town, on some errand or other. Needless to say, when it was time for the return journey, the aircraft proved to be unserviceable, and so I was detailed to fly an Air Engineer Officer and an Air Artificer to the rescue. As usual at that time of the year, the region was enjoying beautiful weather and I flew low level all the way, all three of us thoroughly enjoying the changing scenery. At Port Elizabeth we had to wait overnight for repairs to be completed and next day we set off back to Wingfield. As we were flying sedately along we came to a town called George with an airfield on the outskirts—and, lo and behold, there was a Seafire on the ground. We flew round at low level, having established that it was ours, I landed and the two engineers leapt out to find out what had gone wrong. They estimated that repairs would take about three hours.

The Seafire pilot and I decided to go down to the beach for a walk. It was absolutely beautiful—wide, golden sands, lovely blue sea with waves about three feet high breaking all along, and completely deserted. We decided to go 'skinny dipping'. The water was not too cold and we found that the waves were strong enough for us to be carried in, surfing without a board, right on to the beach. We were thoroughly enjoying ourselves swimming out and being carried back in again when we saw a family walking along the beach to watch us. Instead of surfing in to be delivered naked at their feet, we had to potter around in the waves until they got bored and wandered off. Then we dried off in the sun, dressed and wandered back to the airfield. Finding that the Seafire was once again serviceable, we flew off back to base.

A week later, we were given fourteen days' leave and we found that there were a number of invitations from families prepared to look after us at no cost to ourselves. My friend Bob White and I accepted an invitation from a family in Johannesburg and were given travel warrants from Cape Town by the Blue Train. This was one of the world famous train journeys of the time and we felt tremendously privileged. Its reputation was fully justified, and we were treated royally: it was a most memorable overnight journey.

On arrival at Jo'burg we were met by a driver who took us to a large office building in the city, where we met our host, a Mr J.M. Osborne. He was the Managing Director of Dorman Long (South Africa) Ltd, one of the biggest steel companies in the country. He gave us lunch at his club and arranged for us to be shown around the city in the afternoon. Then he took us to his home, a huge mansion in beautiful gardens, a large swimming pool and tennis courts, all walled in with ornate, guarded gates. His wife was charming and made us feel most welcome and he had two delightful daughters both of whom were in our age group. The girls organised our evenings and social activities while our days were spent seeing as much as possible of the city and surroundings. We were not allowed to pay for anything: all was given to us, most generously.

One visit which did really impress us was that to Pretoria and, while we were there, being taken down the Robinson Deep Gold Mine, at 9,400 feet one of the deepest in the country. It was fascinating to see and experience the conditions under which the natives worked; the temperature was, for us, absolutely strength-sapping. Sadly, with the passage of time, too many of the details have faded away, but I can remember that it was truly a fabulous holiday.

During this time some of our aircrews and many of our ratings were leaving and others were being warned of having dates in the future for demobilisation, or 'demob'. My name had not yet been mentioned. Before I joined the Service, I had been an apprentice brewer in my home town of Alloa in Scotland. The company I was working for was owned by Ind Coope and Allsopp, and when I had left to join up the company had decided to pay me a retainer throughout my naval career, so I did feel an obligation to return to them after my demob. I had reluctantly turned down two offers of jobs, one in Jo'burg and the other in Cape Town, and so, when my chum Peter Cane said that he was thinking of applying for a four-year, short-term commission in the RN with the possibility of a permanent commission at the end of it, I volunteered to take his place and go home after *Colossus* returned to Ceylon.

This was arranged, and my last Barracuda flight with 827 Squadron was flying ashore to Katukurunda on 27 April 1946, after accumulating 395 hours and 73 deck landings by day and night.

Accepting that the aircraft was, unfortunately, underpowered because of other wartime priorities, it had served me very well throughout my twenty-seven months of flying in climates from arctic to tropical, from shore and carrier-borne, by day and by night, and had been most forgiving of my many mistakes with the exception of my major error on 26 April 1944. Even then, it had allowed me to get out in time, so I have no complaints at all. I enjoyed many exciting times with my observer, Bob Smith, who was sadly killed in an aircraft accident just after the war, and my telegraphist air gunner, Ron Hibbs, whose personal friendship I treasured until his death on Good Friday 2010.

Left, above and right: Three more photographs taken over the Cape landscape. Compared with the intensity of the previous six years, these were carefree days indeed. The photograph above depicts PM821/'374', the author's aircraft—i.e., the 827 Squadron Barracuda that he, whenever possible, flew personally (although it so happens that in this instance it is being flown by Squadron colleague Sub-Lieutenant J. Stark RNVR). Notice the aircraft's well-scuffed appearance, the overpainted wing leading edges and nose panelling, the replacement port wing tip and the deletion of the radar array. Though not visible here, the observer's blister windows have also been removed, and replaced with sheet Perspex (this modification is discernible in the original photograph of '376' at right). Interestingly, published production lists state that all PM- and PN-serialled Barracudas were (Fairey-built) Mk IIIs; several examples from these blocks are illustrated in this book. However, many if not most of these aircraft were, in fact, Mk IIs.

BARRACUDA

Hunting Bibers *Commander Andy Phillip*

After completing my operational flying at Ronaldsway in the Isle of Man, I and my crew—Petty Officer Tyler and Leading Airman Shaw—were appointed to join 810 Squadron at RAF Thorney Island in December 1944. At the time, the Squadron was flying the Barracuda Mk II but the following February it re-equipped with the Mk III. The upgraded aircraft was fitted with ASV Mk XI 3cm radar, which had a fully rotatable scanner and the fairly new magnetron, giving, supposedly, much enhanced detection of small objects.

We flew some anti-submarine patrols, each of three hours' duration or more, off the coast of northern France, staying ten miles offshore. During the time 810 were at Thorney I do not recall hearing of any Squadron member getting a detection on a U-boat with radar, or indeed with the Mark One Eyeball; in fact, we saw nothing of interest.

On 9 April 1945 the Squadron, under the command of Lieutenant-Commander Percy Heath RN, moved to RAF Beccles in Norfolk with eighteen aircraft, tasked with the duties of anti-submarine and anti-small-battle-unit patrol, detection and minelaying. The reason for the move to Beccles was the growing menace of midget submarines operating off the East Coast and off the Scheldt estuary, causing some problems with shipping from East Anglian ports to the Low Countries. The midget submarines were the 'Biber' type, two-man submarines fitted with two mines and powered by a petrol engine giving a speed of about 5–6 knots; and the 'Seehund' type—developed, I believe, from a captured British 'X' craft—which had a two- or three-man crew, were armed with two torpedoes strapped to the sides of the craft and were capable of about nine knots.

The Squadron's aircraft were each equipped with six depth charges, and had an endurance of about four hours. I was fortunate to be on patrol some twenty miles from Lowestoft one day when my pilot saw a 'Biber' on the surface at a range of some four miles. We duly attacked the target and saw oil rise to the surface, but, having been on patrol for three hours, we called for assistance and were relieved by another aircraft to keep the submarine down. What we did not realise was that, because of the craft's petrol engine, the last resort for the German crew was to dive and to use the engine, as this caused carbon monoxide poisoning. Some three days after our attack a mini submarine was found abandoned and was towed into Lowestoft.

Flying to and from RAF Beccles had its complications. With radio silence in force, it was essential to listen extremely carefully to the pre-flight briefing. The 24-hour day was divided into four-hour segments, each segment having it own two-figure code and its own coloured flare;

Above and below: The Barracuda Mk III, immediately distinguishable by virtue of the large radome mounted beneath the rear fuselage, was widely employed in the anti-submarine rôle well into the postwar years. Production was shared between Fairey and Boulton Paul.

for example, noon to four might have code 'AB' and a flare of red-yellow-red. The next four hours, four to eight, might be 'TZ' with the cartridge yellow-yellow-red. Re-entry to Beccles was via a narrow gate some one and a half miles either side of Southwold lighthouse, and we then flew over to a beacon (with the code), which was also movable: on a set bearing and distance from the Southwold lighthouse, this beacon was at a known distance and bearing from Beccles airfield. The code was changed every four hours.

Keeping in mind that the home anti-aircraft gunners were trigger-happy, on your re-entry you had to have the right colour cartridge in the Very pistol, the right code, and the correct bearing and distance from the lighthouse and,

Above: A bit of a mess at RNAS Machrihanish involving two Barracudas, the nearest a Mk III believed to be from 810 Squadron. Firefighters have been in attendance and foam covers much of the scene, but evidently the conflagration has now been left to burn out.

again, the correct bearing and distance from the beacon to the airfield. It can be imagined that the observer had to be on the ball—more so if the flight overlapped two of the time segments and the necessary changes that happened during the flight. With so many airfields in East Anglia, strict observance of the above re-entry was essential, firstly to avoid landing at the wrong airfield, and secondly to allow the aircraft at other airfields clear landing space. With all of the above on top of the operational briefing, there was, at times quite a handful to take on board.

The Squadron had some other successes. At least one 'Seehund', another 'Biber' and some small enemy inshore craft were claimed as sunk. We continued flying up to VE-Day, when we were granted five days' leave. We returned to Beccles, but in early June the Squadron moved to Machrihanish for a pre-carrier work-up, the pilots concentrating on deck landing practice and dummy depth-charge dropping whilst the observers had a quick course on the expendable radio sonobuoy.

This last was an American invention which was used to track a submerged submarine from a possible sighting. The buoy, some two feet long and with a diameter of about five inches, consisted of a flotation chamber containing electronics and a chamber which housed the hydrophone and its associated thirty feet of cable. There were six sonobuoys to a complete set, each buoy having its own specific radio frequency and distinctive colour. A radio receiver in the observer's cockpit had a special dial with six segments marked with the colours of the buoys, and by turning the dial to one of the colours the observer would hear the frequency of that particular buoy. In operation, the aim was to drop a smoke float and a sonobuoy on the last known place where the submarine had dived, trying to anticipate the probable track of the dive. A second buoy was dropped 1,000 yards in the presumed direction of the dive. Meanwhile the observer was tuning into the coloured segments of the buoys that were being dropped. If nothing was heard, the observer could lay an extended pattern of buoys in the hope of gaining a contact.

In 1945 all sonobuoys were passive, in that they merely detected sounds—which usually meant propeller noises—and their operating life was about 90–100 minutes, after which the soluble plug gave way and the device sank. The operating procedures established at that time are still in use with the Fleet Air Arm's A/S squadrons today, although of course great technical advances in underwater detection using a very comprehensive range of sophisticated active and passive buoys have been made in the intervening years.

On 10 August the squadron embarked on HMS *Queen* and set sail for the Far East, but the dropping of the second atom bomb resulted in the carrier being recalled and we disembarked, the aircraft going to Machrihanish and the rest of crews going on extended leave. I, however, was sent to RNAS Drem to start a Night Fighter Course with 796 Squadron on Firefly Mk Is fitted with AN/APS-4 radar.

Left: Deck landing practice (DLP) brought its hiccoughs, as this photograph of a Barracuda II—flown by 810 Squadron though retaining 769 Squadron coding—tipping over the side on board HMS *Queen* demonstrates. It looks as if the censor started to blot out the ASV array but then changed his mind.

Katukurunda Etcetera *Petty Officer Roland Spiller*

The Barracuda, I recall, was not particularly loved by its aircrews. It was a faster aircraft compared to the Swordfish and Albacore but it seemed to require much greater concentration when in the air. It was a fairly comfortable aircraft to fly, although though the 'greenhouse effect' of the cockpit canopy could be dangerous; indeed, as a Telegraphist Air Gunner, I suffered badly from sunburn on one occasion while flying in India.

I cannot recall the communication equipment of the Barracuda in much detail. The main set was the 'Wurlitzer' —bulky but workable unless you had to change frequency coils in flight. The wireless set was positioned below the gun mounting. There was also an IFF set, sometimes switched on unknowingly and thereby upsetting the ships' radar. The radar set was sited just below the TAG's seat but he was not always provided with a tube to look at. The aerial display was the 'battleship' array. On the whole the radar was reliable, though if it was not working to one's satisfaction it was sometimes necessary to give it a kick. Around the sides of the TAG's position were full magazines of 0.303 ammunition: if I remember correctly, there were three ball, one incendiary and one tracer. I never fired in action. For the raid on Sigli (Sumatra) I was given a camera so that I could take photographs of things that were interesting. However, when I pulled back the TAG canopy to get a good shot, whilst in a dive, the pilot, Lieutenant Black, insisted that I closed it again as it was disturbing the flow of the aircraft. The intercom system was not, I feel, designed to assist the TAG when he was transmitting: there was nothing worse than the pilot and the observer chattering to each other when he was attempting to record a message that was being received!

TAGs usually started on operations in the rank of Leading Airman (equivalent to RAF Corporal) and as such did not have an Aircrew Mess. The life of aircrew was quite boring at times: if you were not flying there was not a lot to do. Perhaps Morse practice?

Having been flying Albacores on board HMS *Furious*, 822 Squadron moved to Lee-on-Solent in July 1943 and commenced work-up on Barracuda IIs. My first flight in the aircraft took place on 31 August 1943 and it was not the best introduction to a new experience: the pilot, Lieutenant Crane, decided to attempt some fighter evasion manoeuvres whilst I was adjusting the wireless set and I was stuck with my head jammed in a rather uncomfortable position until he had finished! The CO at this time was Lieutenant-Commander Boulding, who had flown Hurricanes from catapult-armed merchant ships. He was used to landing in the sea. Another unpromising clue came in the following month, September, when the Squadron photographer took

Below: A Barracuda is recovered in board HMS *Victorious* after its undercarriage collapsed on landing. The national markings have been repainted in somewhat makeshift fashion in order to obliterate the red centres, in keeping with service requirements in the Far East. Notice, too, the detached starboard wing tip, and the strips of fabric stuck over the gap between the wing tip and the wing proper—a 'field modification' common on Barracudas.

our pictures. When asked why, he replied, 'In case you get killed. We can send the picture to the local press.' Over the next few weeks we carried out four ALTs (in reality, attacks with smoke bombs).

We remained at Lee-on-Solent until the end of October, and before we moved on many of the longer serving aircrew of the Squadron were sent to a quieter job, some taking the TAG 2 Course.

On 15 and 16 November 1943 the Squadron moved to Tain in Scotland, an RAF station. The journey was via RAF Croft, where we stayed overnight, and then via RNAS Arbroath for refuelling. We remained at Tain under the command of Lieutenant-Commander G. A. Woods RNVR, an observer; the Senior Observer was Lieutenant H. Wild RNVR. It was during this time that the Wing Leader was Lieutenant-Commander G. Douglas RNR DFC—the latter an unusual decoration for a Navy flyer and one that was, I believe, awarded for attacks on E-boats while flying from RAF Manston. We flew a large number of ALTs; in fact, we were renowned for our accuracy in dropping them. We also dropped dummy torpedoes using the old four-stack, ex-US destroyer HMS *Reading* as a target ship.

Similar exercises continued through to the New Year, and in February 1944 we left Tain for RNAS Crail for the final drops. Then on 18 February we flew to RNAS Burscough in Lancashire and on the 29th flew to Renfrew and left our aircraft there. The Squadron then moved to Liverpool and took passage on the SS *Strathnaver*. At the dockside there was also the *Louis Pasteur* and the *Rienna del Pacifico*, both of which we would have liked to have boarded as they were on the US run.

We sailed on the *Strathnaver* to Port Said and then transferred to a coal-burning ex-Pilgrim ship. It was an experience I would not like to repeat. For most of March we were at sea, finally discovering that we were bound for India. The Squadron's aircraft were ferried out on board two escort carriers (one of which was HMS *Atheling*) and delivered to St Thomas Mount near Madras for onward flight to Ulunderpet. When we arrived at Ulunderpet we found our aircraft ready and with their torpedoes fully charged. It seems that we were to form part of the defence of India, pitted against the Japanese fleet. Luckily that fleet never arrived.

Ulunderpet (now an Indian Air Force base) was quite remote and there were no large towns nearby. Our 'run ashore' was to Pondicherry in French India. The accommodation on the Station was primitive as we lived in basha huts open both to the weather and to thieves. The huts were hazardous, a fact that became plain to all when those housing 815 and 817 Squadrons, also at Ulunderpet, caught fire, causing some damage and losses.

In April/May 1944 the Senior 'O' was Lieutenant Harsant RNVR, who had been on board HMS *Edinburgh* when she was torpedoed by a U-boat while carrying Russian gold. Early in May we moved to China Bay near Trincomalee, chiefly for more torpedo practice using HMS *Eritrea* as the target ship. It was here that I flew as crew for one trip to Sub-Lieutenant 'Doc' Hadley, author of *Barracuda Pilot*. The following month we moved to Katukurunda (HMS *Ukussa*), the principal Fleet Air Arm base in Ceylon. In terms of flying, we had very little to do though flight tests were undertaken in order to test the Barracuda's endurance in the unaccustomed climate.

Little happened in July 1944 except a night form-up for a carrier landing practice on board *Atheling*, and the month of August was mainly taken up with navigation exercises. September saw one of the few occasions that the Barracuda was used to attack the Japanese, when a raid was mounted on the railway repair yards at Sigli in northern Sumatra.

Left: The picturesque environment at RNAS Katukurunda in Ceylon, where a folded Barracuda II of 756 Squadron, a training and refresher unit, is depicted in about 1944. An Avenger enjoys some rather basic accommodation nearby. As well as serving as a training base and a shore base for disembarked front-line squadrons, Katukurunda also hosted a repair facility and a depôt for aircraft held in reserve.

Right: Loaded with what appear to be three 250-pound bombs, Barracuda '3A' flies to attack Sigli. This is not a good-quality photograph but it is a very interesting image since it is one of the few to show not only the TAG's hood raised while the aircraft is in flight but also his twin machine guns deployed.

Below: The attack on Sigli in northern Sumatra by Barracudas of 815 and 822 Squadrons. Damage was inflicted on railway infrastructure and other targets.

The attack was made by the 45th Wing, consisting of aircraft from 822 Squadron (by now amalgamated with 823 Squadron), flying from HMS *Victorious*, and 815 Squadron (now amalgamated with 817) flying from HMS *Indomitable*. The Wing Leader was Lieutenant-Commander Britton, known to all as 'Horsey'. There were no losses on this raid, but one aircraft crashed on landing on the 'Indom'. My own aircraft, while I was preparing it for the raid, was taken from me in a hurry. The new crew took off and dived straight into the sea, though luckily they were all picked up. It transpired that the petrol had become contaminated with sea water (used for ballasting the ship's tanks). However, the mechanics did a marvellous job in clearing the aircraft's tanks and thanks to their hard work the raid was able to proceed.

On 21 September 1944 I flew in a Barracuda for the last time. The Squadron was closed down at Katukurunda and the crews dispersed, some going home and some moving on to the British Pacific Fleet I was sent back to Britain. On reflection it was not an exciting time, and my thoughts as to the waste of resources, plus the hours and the cost of training involved, probably do not bear repeating.

On the whole I found the 'Barra' to be a safe and comfortable aircraft. Had it been fitted with the original engine, the Exe, many of its early problems might have been overcome. It is worth remembering that the Barracuda, when loaded with a torpedo, was faster than the Swordfish and Albacore but had much the same maximum flying ceiling.

The last time that I can recall of seeing this aircraft in flight was when I was at Lisahally submarine base on Lough Foyle, Londonderry. This was on the day when the U-boats were surrendering: they came up the Foyle and a squadron formation of Barracudas (probably from Eglinton) flew overhead, having been preceded by a squadron formation of Swordfish (no doubt from 836 Squadron at Maydown, where I was stationed at the time).

Change of Plan *Lieutenant (A) John Dickson RD RNVR*

Back on board, we left Malta on 22 May 1945, eastwards through the Med to Port Said. A couple of days were spent ashore in Alexandria. We proceeded down through the Suez Canal, leaving Aden off to port after we had sailed down the Red Sea. On 9 June we arrived off Ceylon. We were accelerated off the deck very early and landed at Trincomalee on the north-east coast, where we had breakfast. The climate here was dry and hot. We were soon airborne again, now flying south-west across the island to RNAS Katukurunda (HMS *Ukussa*) through a violently turbulent tropical storm en route—it was a miracle that we stayed in formation. On this side of Ceylon the climate is hot, sticky, humid and horrible—and we were here for a month. We didn't do very much flying while we were at Katukurunda but we were fitted with RATOG, which produced lots of smoke and sparks but was not terribly efficient. The idea was to enable us to get off the deck with a useful load in the high temperatures.

It must have been about this time that our future was again put in doubt. There were rumours of *Vengeance*, *Venerable*, *Colossus* and *Glory* joining the East Indies Fleet, ready for the invasions of Rangoon and Singapore. However, bearing in mind the poor performance of Barracudas in these climates a year or two earlier, it wasn't surprising that we weren't wanted. It was obvious that our rôle was changing. Meanwhile we shed a few more aircrew, notably 'Bambi' Brook (my observer), Bill Broad and Joe Spencer. On 4 July we flew all aircraft back on board and after a day or two in Colombo sailed round to China Bay and thence, on the 7th, to Australia.

On 11 July, half way across the Indian Ocean, we took off with RATOG, covering all and sundry with smoke and sparks. We carried out a mock attack on the Cocos Islands while the Corsair boys practised their photo-reconnaissance skills taking pictures of the native girls on the beaches in their grass skirts. Two days later we practised dive bombing with long-range fuel tanks attached.

The ship anchored off Fremantle on the 16th but we did not go ashore. On through the Australian Bight, and at first light on 22 July, while still miles out at sea, we smelt the eucalyptus and gum trees—a wonderful change and the promise of happier days ashore.

Later that day we flew off to Jervis Bay, about eighty miles south of Sydney. This was an RAAF airstrip taken over by the Navy and commissioned as HMS *Nabswick* (otherwise Mobile Naval Air Base 5, or MONAB 5). We had left three aircraft behind when we flew off, but by the time the ship anchored in the Bay that afternoon they had been mended, and, as the Captain did not want them cluttering up his deck, three of us were taken by launch back on board and told to fly them off. It seemed the Captain had no thought of raising the anchor and steaming out to give us a fair wind over the deck: instead, we were told we could be boosted off while the ship stayed firmly at anchor. This did not seem a good idea to me, particularly as I had drawn the short straw and was due off first. Johnny Cookson and 'Robbie' Burns thought they could reasonably refuse if they saw me swimming! Anyway, they wound the catapult up to the 'overboost' notch and off I went, well blacked out. By the time I opened my eyes I was over the edge of the airfield, so I just landed, never having retracted the undercarriage. It must have been the shortest recorded

Below: Barracudas of 812 Squadron packed cheek-by-jowl in the hangar on board HMS *Vengeance*, on duty in Far Eastern waters. Notice the spares hung along the far hangar wall. The efficient stowage of aircraft below called for skill and experience on the part of the handlers.

Above: 812 Squadron's Barracuda '380'—possibly MX653—on the point of being boosted for take-off on board *Vengeance*. As may be seen from other photographs throughout this book, the cradle attachment points on the fuselage were very prominent.

flight since that of the Wright Brothers in 1903. Flying was very spasmodic, mainly consisting of ferrying old and new aircraft, respectively to and from the holding pool at Bankstown (MONAB 2, or HMS *Nabberley*) on the outskirts of Sydney. I marvelled at the rows and rows of brand new aircraft from the United States, all pristine in the 'midnight blue' paint finish of the British Pacific Fleet, shining in the warm sunshine. These were Hellcats, Corsairs and Avengers. The Barracudas were also to be found, almost out of sight in the rearmost rank!

The ship was in dock in Sydney having new anti-aircraft guns fitted and we all had a week's leave. We lived on board and sampled the delights of the beaches and city as we pleased. On 8 August I was on a train going back to Jervis Bay when I saw newspaper headlines about the atomic bomb on Hiroshima two days earlier. The next day the second bomb dropped on Nagasaki. The war ended on 15 August and the world was, finally, at peace.

So there we were, probably the most worked up and highly trained squadron never to have fired a shot in anger. This had been achieved over an intensive fourteen-and-a-half-month period, and, sadly, ten of our good chums did not live to see the day and Harry Saggs had a broken back. Of much less importance, we had ditched, wrecked or at least heavily damaged at least twice that number of His Majesty's aircraft.

On 13 August, two days before VJ-Day, I had flown back on board with 'Stormy' Fairweather as passenger and 'Kid' Attenburrow, and one of the Corsair pilots clocked up the ship's one-thousandth deck landing. On 14 August we anchored in Sydney harbour and that night enjoyed a run ashore.

On the historic day the skies were blue, the sun shone and there were puffy white clouds. We were anchored close enough inshore to hear the bands playing, and from the noise of the ships sirens there was obviously a huge party brewing. 'Clear lower deck' was piped and the whole ship's company, in smartest uniforms, fell in on the flight deck. Admiral Harcourt came aboard and gave us a chat. We were expecting, 'Well done everyone, splice the mainbrace and take a couple of days' leave.' Instead we got, 'Well done everyone, you can splice the mainbrace in a couple of days when you get to Manus and you're sailing this afternoon.' There could have been a riot, and one or two suggested jumping overboard and swimming ashore, but sanity prevailed and we slunk below to drown our sorrows.

In the afternoon we weighed anchor and sailed north in company with *Colossus*, the cruiser *Bermuda* and three destroyers. Leaving the fireworks and fun behind, we sailed at top speed (why?). The next day there was a concert in the hangar, and on the 17th we took off and carried out a dummy attack on the Fleet although we wondered for what purpose. Tom Stacey flew his Corsair through both barriers when landing-on and messed up a couple of others but no one got hurt. We sailed on past New Guinea, New Britain and the Coral Islands, finally dropping anchor off Manus in the Admiralties in the morning of 20 August. We spent the rest of the day fuelling.

Colossus and *Bermuda* sailed away but we just sat there. Manus seemed like hell on earth—hot, sticky and humid, and with no breeze, and with very little to tempt us ashore. We did splice the mainbrace, but how much sweeter it would have tasted back in Sydney!

On the 23rd we put to sea for a day, mainly to get some air through the ship. We flew off, I in MX695, but my engine was rough so I landed back on after only twenty minutes. The next day I was ashore with 'Robbie' Burns but we were nearly drowned in a monsoon. After a week which we all thought could have been better spent in Sydney, we flew off using RATOG, loaded with 500-pound bombs which we proceeded to drop on some isolated rock. I think the Commander was trying to empty the ship's magazines so that the space could be otherwise used. Ponam Island was just a large lump of coral where the Americans had flattened a long strip into a runway. It now rejoiced in the name of HMS *Nabaron*, otherwise MONAB 4. I remember there were some Vultee Vengeance dive bombers of 721 Squadron present. They had only ever been used for towing targets and now they were engaged in spraying DDT on the mosquitoes.

We spent two days swimming in the lagoon and organising crab races on the beach. At last, on 30 August, we sailed for Leyte in the Philippines. Meanwhile *Venerable* had got to Hong Kong and *Glory* had reached Rabaul in New Guinea. We crossed the Equator on the 30th and dropped anchor at Leyte on 2 September, where we refuelled and re-provisioned and then sailed immediately. *Colossus* and *Bermuda* were also at Leyte, prior to sailing for Shanghai.

After a pleasant two-day cruise through the Philippines, we arrived in Hong Kong harbour on the 5th. Already there were the carriers *Indomitable*, *Venerable* and *Vindex*, the battleship *Anson*, the cruisers *Swiftsure* and *Euryalus*, the supply ship *Maidstone*, the troopship *Empress of Australia* and many other vessels. The British were back.

We in 812 Squadron did not fly for nearly five weeks after arriving in Hong Kong. The place had been pretty well bombed by the Americans, and it was a smelly, dirty shambles with a good deal of rubble strewn around. It soon became clear that we were to be here for some while and, as there would be no flying, jobs were found for us ashore. The restitution of law and order was the main priority, and our sailors were quickly armed and made up into patrols to clean up the streets. There had been massive looting, and I remember going into a luxurious mansion well up on the Peak and finding little standing apart from the walls and roof. All the woodwork, including floors and doors, had been stripped. I also looked at a small factory where all the machinery was a tangled mess and all the plumbing and electric wiring had gone. The Japanese prisoners were still a problem even after they had been rounded up. A few still felt disgrace and humiliation at being captured and preferred to commit *hara-kiri*. Our troops were forced to make comprehensive searches of their kit to ensure that no lethal weapons were concealed. No matter how we tried, a few still found ingenious ways of ending their lives.

Vengeance put to sea on 1 October and two days later the Corsairs of 1850 Squadron flew ashore to Kai Tak airfield, which became HMS *Nabcatcher* or MONAB 8. I seem to remember that the Corsairs were given a free rein to 'show the flag', and they had the time of their lives screaming around the Colony at low level. The ship returned to harbour on 4 October, when those of us who had been living ashore like gypsies 'walked' back on board. 812 Squadron took off on 8 October and flew in formation to Kai Tak, 'showing the flag' en route. My logbook shows Sub-Lieutenant 'Bill' Williams as observer plus two passengers. The latter must have been very small and very uncomfortable. The next day we took part in the Victory Fly Past over Hong Kong. Included with the Corsairs and Barracudas (the latter from both 812 and 814 Squadrons) were RAF Spitfires that had recently flown in from Burma. It must have been a quite impressive sight.

We were now to live under canvas in the middle of Kai Tak airfield. Fifty years on, one marvels at the thought: imagine a tented camp in the middle of Heathrow! For nearly three months until we left Hong Kong at the end of December we flew very intensively. There were border patrols, mine searches in the harbour entrances, anti-piracy patrols and close-formation flying for photography, while dive-bombing with 25-pounders on Table Island and on a rock known as Gau Tau cropped up very frequently. Commandos made an anti-piracy landing on Ping Chau island and we gave low-level support—albeit without weapons! Ships arriving and leaving harbour were 'attacked' and then photographed from low altitude. *Black Prince* (a new cruiser), *Implacable*, *Glory* and the destroyer *Kempenfeld* all received our attention.

A few trips from all the flying we did over the following ten weeks linger in the memory. PN120, a late-model Barracuda, became 'my' aircraft, and down over Macao (still a

Left: 812 Squadron's MX795, sporting a ferocious looking 'big bad wolf' cartoon character chewing on a bomb (and a primed, replacement engine panel) about to be accelerated off *Vengeance*. The Flight Deck Officer (foreground) and the Flight Deck Engineer Officer are signalling to the pilot (perhaps Sub-Lieutenant Reg Parton—this Barracuda was 'his' aircraft, which sometime also sported 'Goofy' in the port side) that everything is ready, and he is opening the throttle. Opposite, top: HMS *Vengeance* arrived in Hong Kong on 5 September 1945 and, given the work required to re-establish the British presence there, 812 Squadron personnel were detailed to assist. The aircraft were not required for some weeks and remained embarked. Here PM949 has been securely lashed down to the flight deck aft.

Portuguese colony) I put it through its paces—to the extent of performing loops and spins! I ferried a couple of US Navy ratings on a tour of the New Territories, and the next day, with another passenger on board, I proceeded to get lost as the homing beacon was out of action. We had been sight-seeing over all the beautiful little bays and inlets which lie north of the eastern entrance to the harbour, but the maps in those days were sketchy to say the least. There was a sigh of relief when we made it back just as the bar was opening. The flight home into the most spectacular sunset remains a vivid memory.

On 16 November I was briefed to fly two VIPs to White Cloud airfield in Canton, in that part of China ruled by the Nationalists. Although the latter were supposedly our allies, there was severe political tension and it seemed that my Barracuda intruding into their air space might have been interpreted as a sign of colonial expansion by the Imperialist British. I was warned to be careful, and just to be on the safe side I was given an escort of two Corsairs. The two passengers turned out to be a bishop and his chaplain. Neither was very sensibly dressed for riding in the back seats of a Barracuda, and they seemed very tight-lipped when I went through the emergency procedures and showed them how to communicate. In the event I don't think we exchanged one word from beginning to end; I assumed that they would rely on Divine Intervention should we experience a problem. White Cloud airport was basic to say the least, with no runways and precious little grass on a dry, dusty field. The Corsairs circled overhead while I landed and, sure enough, I was confronted by several troops waving and pointing sub-machine guns in my direction. They signalled that I should not switch off, so the two reverend gentlemen had to disembark in the slipstream with the dust blowing up their garments—all most undignified. I was airborne again as quickly as possible. The Corsairs decided to fly back down the Pearl River at low level to the consternation of numerous junks which surely had the right of way, and I followed meekly in their wake.

Don Cawley, a paratroop officer just in from Burma, whom we had befriended, loved flying, so whenever his army duties allowed he would scrounge a ride in any back seat that was unoccupied. On 15 October I was guilty of bad judgment and poor discipline. Don and Bill Williams, my observer at the time, were in the back seats and our brief was border patrol and mine search. I thought it would be a good opportunity to say 'Good morning' to Olga (later to become Mrs Cawley) and another of our lady friends whom we had met whilst ashore and who were employed as stenographers in Government departments occupying part of the Peninsula Hotel. I knew one of the ladies worked in an office on the fourth floor overlooking the harbour so we flew past her window waving like mad. Sadly, we must have badly frightened the passers-by on the Strand and many more waiting to board the Star Ferry at the nearby jetty. On reflection it was a stupid thing to do, and youthful high spirits could be no excuse.

Retribution came in the form of a Canadian colonel who, I was told, was shaving in his room on the fifth floor when an aircraft flew by beneath him. It could be that he cut himself; be that as it may, he was quick enough to spot my aircraft's number, which was duly reported to the Captain at Kai Tak with the recommendation that the stupid pilot be court martialled. On landing I was told to present myself to Captain Surtees DSO RN, who warned me that a court martial could be set up once the Canadian colonel had presented details of what he had seen. However, I was not put under any sort of arrest and I was not stopped from flying, neither was I 'confined to barracks'. Even more humiliating was the reaction of the ladies, who, far from being impressed, thought the whole episode stupid, frightening and childish. The threat of a court martial dampened my spirits for a couple of weeks and then Captain Surtees told me that my misdemeanour had been referred to Captain Neame DSO RN, our ship's captain, who would deal with me once we re-embarked. The final outcome was a dressing down by the Captain, who had all sorts of reports in front of him from, I believe, the Colonel and Captain Surtees, with character references from Captain Tilly and from Cedric Coxon our Squadron CO. Captain Neame endorsed my logbook in red ink and pointed out that a court martial would have meant my staying behind in Hong Kong while the paperwork was sifted but he that had more need of me back on board. My logbook remains quite colourful—red, then green, and finally red.

109

BARRACUDA

Despite the maker's claims, I could only persuade my Barracuda to climb to 18,000 feet. At that altitude it was barely flying, and any attempt to gain a few more feet only resulted in a flat waffle down again. A couple of months later I got a Firefly, which was equipped with a two-stage supercharger, and this took me up to 20,000 feet although the maker's claimed a service ceiling of 29,000.

While the squadrons were ashore the ship went about her business, sailing to Japan and helping with repatriating the prisoners of war. She brought back some thought-provoking photographs of Hiroshima. She had returned at the end of November and I flew back on board on the 29th. There must have been rumours that we would soon discard our Barracudas because 'Mush' Taylor, in an effort to pre-empt the situation, crashed on deck in PM757 the day before. There were no casualties, but there was one less Barracuda. I got airborne off the accelerator loaded with four 250-pound bombs and dive bombed a target towed by the ship (or one thrown over the side). The 'audience' on board seemed pretty impressed. When I landed back on it was to be the last time I flew a Barracuda on to the deck. After lunch we were airborne again and back to Kai Tak. All in all it was quite a busy day.

For the next three weeks we continued flying from the shore base. There were some interesting trips and I recall no untoward incidents. The ship was loading prior to returning to Sydney and because of the deck cargo we couldn't land on. Our aircraft were lightered out and then craned aboard on 21 December.

Our stay in Hong Kong was by this time nearly over. The essential services were all back in business. Telephones were working, the *South China Morning Post* was back in circulation, the Star Ferry was back on schedule, trams were running and the harbour was alive with merchant shipping from around the world. The public buildings and streets still needed major repairs, but when we sailed out on 28 December it was with the satisfaction of a job well done.

Above: Barracuda fly past: half a dozen 812 Squadron Barracudas over Kai Tak, 14 December 1945.

812 last flew its Barracudas on 12 January 1946 when Cedric Coxon led us off the deck of *Vengeance* to Schofields (otherwise MONAB 6, HMS *Nabstock*), just north of Sydney, where we awaited the Fireflies with which we would soon be re-equipped. PN120 had served me well during its short life, and it was nice to have Petty Officer 'Pip' Piper, one of our original crew members, in my back seat on this somewhat nostalgic occasion.

Below: HMS *Vengeance* in Far Eastern waters, with 812 Squadron Barracudas ranged on the flight deck aft. The ship in painted according to the Admiralty Standard Scheme Type B—commonly seen on vessels serving in the Far East towards the end of the war—which featured a dark grey panel extending over much of the length of the hull.

A Little Observation *Lieutenant Keith Davies*

After six months' initial naval training in HMS *Indefatigable*, based at Portland, I joined the Observer School at RNAS St Merryn, near Padstow in Cornwall, on 14 May 1952. Excitement rose as we were issued with our flying gear and equipment, including the Bigsworth board, a sophisticated parallel-arm drawing board twenty inches square to which a navigation chart could be attached with spring clips, and which was accompanied by a Course Setting Calculator (CSC). These were stowed and carried in a canvas holdall into which all other necessary items—pencils, rubbers, sharpener and notebooks—were deposited.

750 Squadron was commanded by Lieutenant-Commander Fradd, and Ansons and Barracuda Mk 3s were to provide us with our early flying experiences. These were to learn the basics of navigation, radar operation, and HF wireless transmission at a speed of eighteen words per minute. The operation of radar and general flying practice were carried out in Ansons, in which the 'sprog' observer had the onerous duty of winding up the undercarriage by hand (on take-off in the Barracuda it looked as though the pilot was winding up the undercarriage one wheel at a time as they slowly retracted!). The Barracuda observer's cockpit had plenty of storage space and very good visibility on both sides under the high wing for taking sights on landmarks and bearings on smoke floats when 'finding a wind'.

Navigation exercises could be either 'coastal exercises' or, as the observer became more confident and more accurate, 'sea navigation'. Most exercises departed from and returned to Trevose Head and involved the identification of local coastal features and landfalls, including, as aids to navigation, Land's End, The Lizard, the Scillies and Godrevy Island. Sea navigation, essential of course for carrier operations, often required low-level flying to shadow enemy ships, in which, as the use of VHF to report the position of the target was precluded, the observer would send the report in Morse code in an HF transmission. Also essential in navigation is the ability to appreciate any change in the speed and direction of the wind. The procedure for 'finding a wind' using a smoke float was as follows. The observer called to the pilot, 'Stand by to find a wind, and the pilot, as he set the switch to drop the smoke float, would respond 'Ready'. The observer then called 'Release' as he started his stopwatch in order to time the fall of the float into the sea, telling the pilot to stand by to turn. The pilot was advised 'Turn' as float hit the sea, whereupon he executed a 180-degree Rate 2 turn from the previous course. After 1½ minutes the pilot was told to repeat the same turn to his original course, reporting which side the float was appearing. At three minutes from the start of the first turn a bearing taken on the float gave the wind direction, while times taken when on the beam and on the quarter enabled the speed to be calculated.

Pilots were often very helpful, and would look at the observer's plot before he returned to the crewroom, pointing out any glaring mistakes!

At the end of October 1952 the Course moved on to 796 Squadron to fly Firefly Is. The pilots I flew with in 750 included Lieutenants Aldridge, Bough, Daubney, Davison, Forrest, Marsden, McGregor, Sharp, Stanbridge, Thomas and West and Mr McKerral. The camaraderie and friendship I experienced amongst the aircrew was to be typical of that found throughout the Fleet Air Arm during my eight years of service.

Below: Incident at St Merryn: one fine day in 1950 Barracuda Mk III ME183 of 796 Squadron veered off the runway and came to rest axle-deep in the adjacent turf. The damage was negligible, and the aircraft was swiftly returned to service, eventually (1952) being passed to 750 Squadron with no change of coding.

The Last Hurrah *Lieutenant-Commander David Pennick*

My front-line Fleet Air Arm flying experience began with 703 Squadron and the Fairey Seafox on board the armed merchant cruiser *Canton*, a former passenger liner that had been requisitioned by the Admiralty upon the outbreak of World War II. I trained initially as an observer, and served as such during the war, but latterly served principally as a pilot, having trained for this in order to remain in the Navy with a permanent commission.

815 Squadron was equipped with Barracudas Mk IIIs, operating in the anti-submarine rôle, when the war drew to a close. It disbanded shortly afterwards, but re-formed at RNAS Eglinton, again with Barracuda IIIs, in 1947 for the same purpose. In its new guise it was in fact a renumbered 744 Squadron, which itself had evolved out of 737 NAS. It was now both a potentially operational squadron but it also fulfilled the rôle of a training squadron for anti-submarine work. It fell to me to command the Squadron in an Acting capacity following the tragic death of Lieutenant-Commander David Wynne-Roberts in a climbing accident en route back to RNAS Eglinton following dinghy drill. The appointment came as something of a surprise to me as I was not the most experienced pilot on the Squadron although I was the most senior officer by a couple of years. I was not, to my disappointment, awarded an 'Acting Half'!

815 must have been the most land-bound front-line squadron the Navy ever employed. The Squadron was, in effect, attached to the Joint Anti-Submarine School based at Londonderry; for example, when the School was running a course involving sea-going officers on board A/S vessels, we would provide the air co-operation when they were being trained, or gaining experience, at sea. Individual officers from the School would, on occasion, fly with us in order to broaden their understanding.

In terms of our general activities, as well as sharpening our skills in the anti-submarine rôle we also practised formation flying and worked with land forces on army co-operation duties and other tasks not strictly the remit of an A/S squadron. Anti-submarine work was a central part of the curriculum of course—our Barracudas could often be seen toting mines, smoke floats, sonar buoys or depth charges—but as part of the Joint A/S School we flew under their direction for much of the time, offering the School a pool of experienced aircrew upon which it could call for a variety of tasks to further the training and experience of those attending courses there. We frequently undertook combined exercises with the RN submarine fleet, three or four boats being based at Londonderry for these purposes. In addition, newly commissioned submarines might arrive at Londonderry in the course of their work-up, and 815 would provide experience for the crews in evasion in, and self-protection against, air attack. Both 'sides' of course benefited from these exercises. As part of our training, each

TO BECCLES AND BEYOND

Above: RJ797, a Barracuda Mk III assigned to 815 Squadron, in 1949 or 1950. This is the CO's aircraft, sporting white code letters and numbers rather than the customary black. A Meteor is parked alongside.
Below: Another 815 Squadron Mk III, RJ933, seen in 1952 and with the TAG's side windows sealed off. 'GN' was the tail code for RNAS Eglinton.

aircrew was allocated two live depth charges twice a year. We were never armed with torpedoes, but, curiously, we sometimes practised dummy torpedo attacks on towed targets, and dive-bombing was also prominent on the curriculum.

We went to sea on a number of occasions, one period I remember being on board HMS *Implacable* in May/June 1950 when we took part in an exercise involving some fifteen or twenty ships that included also a light fleet carrier. I found the Barracuda to be a pleasant aircraft to land—very much easier than, for example, the Firefly, in large part due to the pilot's excellent view forward on the approach. It took off very easily, too. We were never obliged to use the accelerator, even when laden with weaponry. We were trained in the use of RATOG but, again, did not employ it operationally when flying the Barracuda.

We normally flew as a three-man aircrew, with the observer and a TAG under the glazing aft of the 'Driver (Airframe)' in the normal manner. The TAG's machine gun armament was retained, but was rarely deployed. Procedures for the crew in the cockpit were little changed in 1950 from wartime days, the observer still relying on his Bigsworth Board, chartboard, pencil and ruler and all the rest, and undertaking essential skills such as wind-finding, but his living space was luxurious in comparison with what had gone before, with far more room and a much improved view out thanks to the large blister windows beneath the wing. The pilot, too, had a very good view from the cockpit—much better, for example, from that from the more modern Firefly. In summary, the Barracuda was quite suitable for the tasks it had to perform in 815, the last frontline FAA unit to operate the type; indeed the Firefly, although it was considerably faster, was, in my view, a much inferior aircraft to the Barracuda in terms of being an effective A/S tool.

113

BARRACUDA

Ben Twitch Tragedy *Commander John Neilson* OBE DSC

After completion of flying training at Lossiemouth I joined *Illustrious* as Ship's Pilot and served there from February until September 1949 before being appointed to 815 (Barracuda) Squadron at Eglinton, Northern Ireland, on 3 October. The airfield was within easy reach of Lough Foyle and the outlet to the Atlantic. To the east of the airfield, and on the approach path to the main runway, was a largish hill dubbed 'Ben Twitch' as it was quite a hazard when one was returning to land at night.

The Barracuda was one of the most ungainly aircraft ever built, with a long, stalky undercarriage with torsion bars that provided a certain amount of lift after take-off so that one had to be careful not to raise the wheels before reaching at least 100 feet for fear of sinking back on to the runway. It had a tendency to suffer from severe mag. drops after start-up, but these could normally be cured by putting out the dive brakes to keep the tail down and running up to about +4 pounds boost.

The aircraft's rôle on 815 Squadron at that time was never quite clear to me as we would alternate between dive bombing and night minelaying. The latter was a most hazardous operation. We would form up in close formation

Below: 815 Squadron Barracuda Mk IIIs on board HMS *Illustrious*—now a training carrier—in 1948. The aircraft are wearing the disruptive camouflage redolent of wartime days; that would soon change.
Bottom: One of the Squadron's Barracudas touches down on board HMS *Indomitable* in June 1951. Five more are parked forward, sandwiched amongst some Blackburn Firebrands of 813 Squadron.

Above: Mk III—or, by now more properly '3'; roman designator numerals were changed to arabic in 1948–RJ924 at Eglinton, with a practice bomb rack installed on its inboard stores station.

and then turn off the navigation lights and simply rely on the tiny wingtip formation lights to keep station before reducing height to 200 feet over the water. Dive bombing was practised from about 5,000 feet in a near-vertical dive (usually about 75 degrees—but feeling like 95!) with dive brakes extended.

Every month we went off by bus to Portrush to the east of Eglinton to practise wet dinghy drill. On one of these occasions we thought it a great idea to have a race up 'Ben Twitch' before returning home. Our boss, Lieutenant-Commander Wynne Roberts, was of course leading but about half way up he slipped and came tumbling down to the bottom. We picked him up and dusted him down before getting him back on the bus. When we got back he wasn't looking too well so we insisted that he went to Sick Bay for a check-up. Next morning at breakfast I asked how the Boss was faring, only to be told in hushed voices that he had passed away during the night from internal injuries.

I suddenly got a pier-head jump off to Malta to join 812 Squadron prior to embarking in HMS *Glory* and sailing on to join the Korean War. My relief was an old course chum of mine, Peter Craig. Part of my brief turnover to him was to tell him about the tendency of the Barracuda to suffer from mag. drops on start-up, but I advised him not to place the aircraft if this happened but just burn it off during a high power run-up with the air brakes out. When I reached Malta I received a letter from him thanking me for my advice. He reported that it had worked just as I predicted, but said that he forgot to retract the air brakes before attempting a take-off. He never left the runway and ended up in the overshoot!

Below: Recovery in progress for Barracuda Mk 3 RJ933 in May 1950, the aircraft having come to grief when its starboard undercarriage collapsed as it was landing at Eglinton. The damage was superficial and the machine was repaired for further service.

BARRACUDA SQUADRONS

SOME sixty Fleet Air Arm squadrons operated the Fairey Barracuda at one time or another, making it one of the most widely employed aircraft ever to serve with the Royal Navy. It was not the last indigenously designed torpedo bomber to be procured for the FAA—the Firebrand and indeed the Wyvern would follow, though these were technically torpedo *fighters*—but it was the last in a long line of 'traditional' three-seat TBR aircraft. In fact, its 'torpedo' rôle—though, as we have seen, vigorously promoted and trained for by aircrews throughout the war—was rarely put into practice during that conflict and by the end of hostilities had to all intents and purposes been abandoned. The Barracuda's employment as a dive bomber was very much more to the point in terms of its value to the Navy, as was its subsequent use as an anti-submarine aircraft.

As described earlier in this book, the introduction of the Barracuda to squadron service was not an entirely trouble-free affair, but once the aircraft's foibles had been addressed and aircrews had begun to get used to its habits, it proved to be a valuable tool, if more so in temperate climes than in tropical (owing to its Merlin engine proving somewhat problematic in hot environments). Its introduction to combat was a relatively low-key, Mediterranean affair, 810 Squadron flying it during the Salerno operation in September 1943. Its days of true glory were to come some seven months later, in April 1944 and subsequently, when it was launched in numbers to attack the German battleship *Tirpitz*, holed up in a Norwegian fjord, first in Operation 'Tungsten' and then, in August that year (and rather less successfully) in the 'Goodwood' raids. At about the same time it was launching attacks on Japanese-held assets in the East Indies, generally in what today would be termed 'interdiction' sorties. Plans for the Barracuda's more widespread use in this theatre

Mk 3 ME293 in service with 796 Squadron—one of the last units to fly the Barracuda. It is finished in the standard FAA colour scheme of Extra Dark Sea Grey and Sky Type 'S', which was introduced in 1948 and was not finally renounced until 1978, when the fleet carrier *Ark Royal* was decommissioned and the Fairey Gannet was withdrawn from service. Interestingly, part of the starboard underwing serial number is carried over on to the leeboard (and presumably this is the case for the port wing also).

were, as recalled in earlier pages, thwarted by the dropping of the atomic bombs by the Americans and the resulting Japanese capitulation.

The aircraft was issued in very large numbers to second-line squadrons, initially for TBR training and conversion purposes and later for anti-submarine training. It was also flown by those units specialising in the various skills peculiar to naval airmanship, for example observer and TAG training, and deck landing training. Additionally, aircraft 'pool' squadrons and refresher training units, plus a number of service trials units, included Barracudas on their inventories.

Although little is recorded of their activities, a number of RAF squadrons were also equipped with the Barracuda, albeit in small numbers. These were employed for the most part in humdrum (yet vital) duties such as anti-aircraft co-operation training, but special mention should be made of No 618 Squadron, the work of which might be deduced from the proximity of the squadron number to that of the 'Dambusters'. The plan was to send Mosquitos equipped with 'Highball' ('bouncing bombs') to the Far East for use against Japanese shipping, and that these aircraft should be flown to their targets off carrier decks. To this end, RAF aircrew assigned to the Squadron underwent carrier deck training in Scotland in 1944, using Barracudas and the escort carrier HMS *Rajah* for the purpose. Until recent years and the formation of the now-defunct Joint Force Harrier, this was one of the very rare instances since the Inskip ruling in 1939 (when the FAA was split off entirely from the RAF) of an RAF unit operating from an aircraft carrier. The deployment of Mosquitos to the Far East was made, incidentally, but in the event they were not used operationally.

BARRACUDA

FRONT-LINE FLEET AIR ARM BARRACUDA SQUADRONS

Unit	Principal location(s)	Commission(s)
810 NAS	RNAS Lee-on-Solent, Machrihanish, Crail and Wingfield, RAF China Bay and Beccles *et alibi* and on board HM Ships *Illustrious* and *Queen*	03/04/33-22/08/45 (Mk IIs 00/04/43-00/07/45, Mk IIIs 00/02/45-00/08/45)
812 NAS	RNAS Stretton, Crail, Burscough, Fearn, Hal Far, Katukurunda *et alibi* and on board HMS *Vengeance*	05/06/44-12/08/46 (Mk IIs 05/06/44-24/01/46)
814 NAS	RNAS Stretton, Hatston, Fearn, Machrihanish, Hal Far, Katukurunda, Kai Tak *et alibi*, and on board HMS *Venerable*	01/07/44-19/11/50 (Mk IIs 01/07/44-00/01/46)
815 NAS	RNAS Lee-on-Solent, RAF Tain, RAF Ulunderpet, RNAS Katukurunda, RNAS Coimbatore, Machrihanish, Fearn and Rattray, *et alibi* and on board HM Ships *Indomitable* and *Smiter*; and (second Barracuda commission) RNAS Eglinton *et alibi* and on board HM Ships *Implacable* and *Indomitable*	01/10/43-11/01/46, 01/12/47-13/10/55 (Mk IIs 01/10/43-00/04/45, Mk IIIs 00/01/45-11/01/46 and 01/12/47-00/05/53)
816 NAS	RNAS Lee-on-Solent, Fearn and Machrihanish	01/02/45-01/07/48 (Mk IIs 01/02/45-00/07/45)
817 NAS	RNAS Lee-on-Solent and Machrihanish, RAF Ulunderpet and China Bay, RNAS Katukurunda, Trincomalee *et alibi* and on board HM Ships *Indomtable* and *Unicorn*; and (second Barracuda commission) RNAS Rattray and Fearn	10/03/41-21/02/45, 01/04/45-23/08/45 (Mk IIs 00/12/43-21/02/45 and 01/04/45-23/08/45)
818 NAS	Located at RNAS Rattray and Fearn	01/05/45-15/08/45 (Mk IIs throughout)

Below: Sub-Lieutenant Ray Taylor makes an unorthodox landing on board HMS *Vengeance* in 812 Squadron's Barracuda II PM757/'381', 28 November 1945 (see page 110). The Squadron was by this time sporting red and white propeller spinners, and notice, too, that the ASV radar equipment has been removed.
Right:: An earlier 'prang' by a Barracuda of 812 Squadron, this one occurring during a landing at RNAS Hal Far, Malta. The accident happened in March 1945, when the Squadron had disembarked from HMS *Vengeance* while working up in the Mediterranean en route to the Far East. The tips of the propeller blades have been neatly removed during the aircraft's two-legged peregrination across the airfield, while the TAG's twin machine guns make a rare appearance in a photograph. By this stage of the war, front-line FAA squadrons were routinely equipped with VHF radio, and the attendant whip antenna can just be seen in this view , to port of the main aerial post.

118

Commanding Officers	Remarks
Lt-Cdr A. J. B. Forde, Lt-Cdr A. G. McWilliam RNVR (27/02/44), Lt-Cdr P. C. Heath (16/12/44)	First squadron to take Barracudas into action (Norway, July 1943); supported landings at Salerno Sept. 1943; Eastern Fleet 1944; coastal patrols SE England 1945.
Lt-Cdr C. R. J. Coxon	To British Pacific Fleet 1945; no offensive action.
Lt-Cdr J. S. L. Crabbe, Lt-Cdr G. R. Coy DSC (29/11/44)	To British Pacific Fleet 1945; no offensive action.
Lt-Cdr R. G. Lawson RNVR, Lt-Cdr D. Norcock (23/12/44), Lt-Cdr J. S. Bailey OBE (05/01/45), Lt-Cdr M. H. Meredith DSC RNVR (18/04/45); Lt-Cdr K. S. Pattisson DSC (01/12/47), Lt-Cdr D. M. R. Wynne-Roberts (01/04/49), Lt D. W. Pennick (01/09/49–Acting), Lt-Cdr C. Murray (15/01/50), Lt-Cdr S. S. Laurie (22/09/50), Lt-Cdr C. R. J. Coxon (12/03/51), Lt-Cdr L. P. Dunne DSC (01/04/52)	To Eastern Fleet 1944 (strikes against enemy infrastructure Aug.–Oct.); returned and re-equipped, then to BPF 1945 (no offensive action). Re-formed as A/S unit Dec. 1947 (renumbered 744 NAS). Last front-line Barracuda squadron.
Lt-Cdr The Hon. W. A. C. Keppel DSC, Lt-Cdr J. S. L. Crabbe (26/06/45)	Re-formed as a Barracuda squadron for service with the BPF but re-equipped with Fireflies after a few months.
Lt-Cdr T. W. May SANF(V); Lt-Cdr M. A. Lacayo (01/04/45)	Re-equipped with Barracudas for service in the Far East and carried out offensive sorties in East Indies Aug.–Oct. 1944. Re-formed Apr. 1945 for service with the BPF but too late to see further action.
Lt-Cdr B. W. Vigrass RNVR	Re-equipped with Barracudas for service in the Far East but too late to be deployed.

continued . . .

Above: A Barracuda of 814 Squadron photographed from the TAG's station in an accompanying aircraft; a third Barracuda can be detected, its port tailplane peeping over the main subject's port flap. Notice that only the after torpedo crutch is present and also, in this photograph and the next, the fabric strips covering the wing-tip joint.

Below: 814 Squadron Barracuda Mk II MX710, having strayed from the flight deck on board HMS *Venerable*, 1945; not much damage done, it appears. The aircraft is still wearing European-theatre national markings, but a directive issued in March that year required that the style for these be changed on those aircraft destined for service with the British Pacific Fleet. The roundels became dark blue and white only, with blue-outlined flanking bars similar to those carried by US Navy aircraft. Wing roundels appeared above the port and below the starboard mainplanes only. Fin flashes were deleted, and a white single letter denoting the carrier on which the aircraft was embarked took their place. BPF Barracudas carried a white, three-letter identity number (referred to as the 'callsign' or 'side number' by personnel) in the range 370–381 (382 for *Colossus*'s aircraft); this number also appeared on the fuselage main undercarriage door, visible from forward when the wheels were down. (This markings scheme is most clearly illustrated in the artwork for the aircraft 'Flown by the Author' on pages 140–141.) Fleet Air Arm aircraft operating with the British Eastern Fleet had already had their markings repainted in order to remove the red elements (see the photographs on pages 103, 123 and elsewhere), to try to prevent 'friendly fire' (Japanese aircraft wore red roundels). The earlier of these directives (issued in September 1943) was fairly liberally interpreted, resulting in a good deal of variation, but the BPF directive was more specific and more rigorous.

Above: An incident on board HMS *Venerable* involving an 814 Squadron Barracuda. The pilot (Sub-Lieutenant Derek Turner) was unhappy with his approach and decided to 'go round again'—although he must have given those in the starboard catwalk something of a fright in the process.

Below: A De Havilland Sea Hornet of 801 Squadron is marshalled into position on board HMS *Implacable*, May 1950. Six more Sea Hornets await their turn to fly, while nine Barracuda Mk 3s of 815 Squadron sit patiently in the background.

Unit	Principal location(s)	Commission(s)
820 NAS	RNAS Lee-on-Solent, Arbroath, Crail, Hatston and Machrihanish and on board HMS *Indefatigable*	01/01/44-16/03/46 (Mk IIs 00/01/44-00/10/44)
821 NAS	RNAS Stretton, Machrihanish, Maydown, Hatston, Fearn, Abbotsinch, Katukurunda, Rattray *et alibi* and on board HM Ships *Puncher* and *Trumpeter*	01/05/44-01/02/46 (Mk IIs until 00/04/45, Mk IIIs from 00/01/45)
822 NAS	RNAS Lee-on-Solent, Tain, Fearn and Crail, RAF Ulunderpet and China Bay, RNAS Katukurunda, Thorney Island, Maydown *et alibi* and on board HM Ships *Atheling* and *Victorious*	5/10/41-19/02/46 (Mk IIs 00/07/43-00/10/44 and 00/06/45-00/09/45, Mk IIIs 00/01/45-00/06/45)
823 NAS	RNAS Lee-on-Solent, Fearn and Burscough, RAF Ulunderpet, RNAS Katukurunda and on board HMS *Atheling*	18/08/33-06/07/44 (Mk IIs 00/06/43-06/07/44)
824 NAS	RNAS Katukurunda and RAF Sulur	02/07/34-04/01/46 (Mk IIs 02/07/45-00/09/45)
825 NAS	RNAS Rattray Head, Fearn and Burscough	01/07/45-01/05/51 (Mk IIs 01/07/45-00/11/45)
826 NAS	RNAS Lee-on-Solent, Crail, Hatston, Grimsetter and Machrihanish and on board HM Ships *Indefatigable* and *Formidable*; and (second Barracuda commission) RNAS East Haven and Fearn	01/12/43-23/10/44, 15/08/45-28/02/46 (Mk IIs 01/12/43-23/10/44 and 15/08/45-00/01/46)

Left: 815 personnel: a formal Squadron photograph taken at Eglinton in 1949. The two Barracuda 3s in the picture are still wearing wartime-style camouflage: notice the colouring of the nose of the aircraft on the left, and the colour demarcation line along the radiator intakes of both aircraft.
Right, upper: Mk II LS503 of 817 Squadron flying in Eastern Fleet markings from HMS *Indomitable* in 1944. The specified style of BEF markings—dark blue and white (or pale blue) roundels, without the flanking panels that would later characterise aircraft assigned to the British Pacific Fleet—is evident in both this and the following photograph.
Right, lower: An 822 Squadron Barracuda makes its getaway from *Atheling*. Here the new markings have been applied in somewhat extemporary fashion over the original European-theatre insignia, and the aircraft's earlier side number appears to have been merely painted out for the present: the constraints of the situation resulted in some very liberal interpretations of 'the rules'.

Commanding Officers	Remarks
Lt-Cdr W. H. Nowell	Took part in Operations 'Mascot' and 'Goodwood' (strikes against *Tirpitz*, July–Aug. 1944) and re-equipped with Avengers shortly thereafter.
Lt-Cdr M. Thorpe, Lt-Cdr D. Brooks DSC* RNVR (14/06/45), Lt-Cdr H. P. Dawson (15/01/46)	TBR sorties 1944, coastal patrol and minelaying Jan.–July 1945. Intended for deployment to Far East but too late to commence operations.
Lt-Cdr P. F. King, Lt-Cdr B. E. Boulding DSC (10/08/43), Lt-Cdr G. A. Woods RNVR (01/12/43), Lt-Cdr L. C. Watson DSC RNVR (13/07/44), Lt-Cdr D. A. Davies DSC RNVR (04/04/45)	Re-equipped with Barracudas for service with the Eastern Fleet; absorbed 823 NAS and flew offensive sorties in East Indies. A/S sorties off British Isles Jan.–May 1945. For deployment to BPF but cancelled with ending of war.
Lt-Cdr G. Douglas RNR, Lt-Cdr L. C. Watson DSC RNVR (01/12/43)	Issued with Barracudas for service with the Eastern Fleet but shortly after arriving in Ceylon was disbanded and integrated into 822 NAS.
Lt G. R. Clarke RNVR, Lt-Cdr S. Brilliant RNVR (10/07/45)	Flew Barracudas for a few weeks in Jul.–Aug. 1945 but returned to Britain on the ending of the war and re-equipped with Fireflies.
Lt-Cdr F. Stovin-Bradford DSC	Flew Barracudas (Canadian aircrews) Jul.–Nov. 1945 but too late to see action.
Lt-Cdr A. J. I. Temple-West, Lt-Cdr S. P. Luke (26/01/44), Lt-Cdr E. S. Carver (15/08/45)	Took part in Operations 'Mascot' and 'Goodwood' and further anti-shipping strikes July–Sep. 1944. RCN-crewed from Aug. 1945.

continued . . .

BARRACUDA

Left, upper: Four officers and all the Telegraphist Air Gunners of 822 Squadron at RNAS Katukurunda, this photograph having been taken after the Squadron had absorbed 823 NAS in July 1944. The CO, Lieutenant-Commander L. C. Watson DSC RNVR, is seated third from the left; our contributor Roland Spiller is seated far left.

Left, lower: An 827 Squadron Barracuda II in British Pacific Fleet markings having come to grief, presumably having suffered a collapsed undercarriage whilst landing (notice the position of the starboard flap).

Opposite, upper left: The aircrews of 830 Squadron, seen on board *Furious* on 25 April 1944. Virtually all present had taken part in 'Tungsten' three weeks earlier; sadly absent are Sub-Lieutenants T. C. Bell and R. N. Drennan and Leading Airman G. J. Burns, who had lost their lives during the operation when their aircraft, '5M', was shot down by the enemy.

Opposite, upper right: Some of the crucial 'back-up boys': air mechanics of 831 Squadron pose with one of their Barracudas.

Opposite, lower: 831 Squadron's complement photographed on the after flight deck of HMS *Victorious* in the summer of 1944 when the ship was serving with the Eastern Fleet. The CO at this time was Lieutenant-Commander J. L. Fisher RNVR.

COLLECTION OF THE LATE LES SAYER

COURTESY DAVID HOBBS

Unit	Principal location(s)	Commission(s)
827 NAS	RNAS Stretton, Machrihanish, Lee-on-Solent, Dunino, Hatston and Donibristle, RAF Beccles and Langham, RNAS Dekheila, Katukurunda, Wingfield *et alibi* and on board HM Ships *Furious*, *Formidable* and *Colossus*	15/09/40–24/07/46 (Mk Is 00/01/43–00/07/43, Mk IIs 00/03/43–00/07/46)
828 NAS	RNAS Lee-on-Solent, Fearn, Machrihanish, Donibristle and Hatston and on board HMS *Implacable*	01/03/44–03/06/46 (Mk IIs 01/03/44–00/02/45)
829 NAS	RNAS Lee-on-Solent, Tain, Machrihanish, Hatston and Burscough and on board HMS *Victorious*	01/10/43–09/07/44 (Mk IIs throughout)
830 NAS	RNAS Lee-on-Solent, Hatston and Donibristle and on board HM Ships *Furious* and *Formidable*	24/05/43–03/10/44 (Mk IIs throughout)
831 NAS	RNAS Lee-on-Solent, Hatston Machrihanish, Maydown, Burscough and Katukurunda and RAF Minneriya and on board HM Ships *Indomitable*, *Victorious* and *Furious*	01/04/41–06/12/44 (Mk Is 00/12/42–00/01/43, Mk IIs 00/01/43–06/12/44)
837 NAS	RNAS Stretton, Lee-on-Solent and Fearn, RAF Ayr, RNAS Katukurunda and RAAF Schofields, Jervis Bay and Nowra and on board HMS *Glory*	01/08/44–06/10/47 (Mk IIs 00/09/44–00/11/45)

BARRACUDA SQUADRONS

Commanding Officers	Remarks
Lt R. W. Little, Lt-Cdr J. S. Bailey (12/03/43), Lt-Cdr R. S. Baker-Falkner DSC (12/08/43), Lt-Cdr K. H. Gibney DSC (25/10/43), Lt-Cdr G. R. Woolston (30/06/44), Lt-Cdr G. R. Clarke (06/07/45), Lt-Cdr L. R. Tivy (16/12/45)	Participated in Operations 'Tungsten', 'Mascot' and 'Goodwood' Apr.–Aug.1944; operations off East Coast (absorbing 830 NAS) Oct.–Dec. 1944. To BPF Mar. 1945 but no offensive sorties.
Lt-Cdr F. A. Swanton DSC	Operations off Norway Oct.–Dec 1944, absorbing 841 NAS. Re-equipped with Avengers Jan. 1945.
Lt-Cdr G. P. C. Williams DSC, Lt-Cdr D. W. Phillips (03/03/44)	Took part in Operation 'Tungsten' and further offensive sorties off Norway Apr.–Jun. 1944. Absorbed into 831 NAS Jul. 1944.
Lt-Cdr F. H. Fox, Lt-Cdr R. D. Kingdon DSC RNVR (21/01/44)	Took part in Operations 'Tungsten' and 'Mascot' and further offensive sorties off Norway Apr.–Jun. 1944. Absorbed into 827 NAS Oct. 1944.
Lt-Cdr A. G. Leatham, Lt-Cdr D. E. C. Eyres (08/05/43), Lt-Cdr E. M. Britton (15/09/43), Lt-Cdr D. Brooks DSC RNVR (13/02/44), Lt-Cdr J. L. Fisher RNVR (06/05/44)	Participated in Operation 'Tungsten' and in anti-shipping strikes off Norway Apr.–Jun. 1944. To Eastern Fleet Jul. 1944; offensive sorties in East Indies until Nov. 1944.
Lt-Cdr R. B. Martin RNVR	For service with BPF Apr. 1945 but arrived in theatre too late to see action.

continued . . .

125

BARRACUDA

Unit	Principal location(s)	Commission(s)
841 NAS	RNAS Lee-on-Solent, Fearn, Machrihanish and Hatston and on board HMS *Implacable*	01/02/44–28/11/44 (Mk IIs throughout)
847 NAS	RNAS Lee-on-Solent, Fearn, Machrihanish and Katukurunda and RAF China Bay and on board HMS *Illustrious*	01/06/43–30/06/44 (Mk IIs throughout)
860 NAS	RAF Ayr and RNAS Fearn and St Merryn and on board HrMS *Karel Doorman*	15/06/43–20/01/46 (Mk IIIs from 00/06/45)

Above: On board HMS *Glory*, an 837 NAS Barracuda demonstrates the results of a heavy arrested landing, the starboard main undercarriage having collapsed. Unusually, the wings have 'C' Type roundels. April or May 1945.

Left: A Barracuda of 837 Squadron is towed aft along the flight deck on board HMS *Glory*. As with the other Barracuda squadrons embarked in the light fleet carriers, 837 saw no action following its arrival in the Far East, and, like them, would quite quickly relinquish its aircraft in favour of Fireflies.

BARRACUDA SQUADRONS

Commanding Officers	Remarks
Lt-Cdr R. J. Fisher RNZNVR, Lt-Cdr E. F. L. Montgomery RNZNVR (01/06/44)	Conducted anti-shipping strikes off Norway. Merged into 828 NAS Nov, 1944.
Lt-Cdr P. C. Whitfield, Lt-Cdr J. L. Cullen (20/07/43)	To Eastern Fleet Dec. 1943; carried out strikes on Japanese-held facilities. Merged into 810 NAS Jun. 1944.
Lt J. van der Toorren RNethN, Lt-Cdr B. Sjerp RNethN (00/01/46)	Dutch-manned. Equipped with Barracudas for six months until replaced by Fireflies.

continued . . .

Above: A collision with HMS *Illustrious*'s island by an unidentified Barracuda of 847 Squadron. An adaptation of the original wing roundels to take account of the directive for FAA aircraft operating with the British Eastern Fleet is clearly evident.

Right: A pair of Dutch Barracudas (860 Squadron) on board the carrier HMS *Nairana* (later transferred to the Royal Netherlands Navy and renamed *Karel Doorman*). Twenty-two Mk IIIs were supplied for deck landing training from stocks relinquished by 822 Squadron, but they served only for six months before being replaced with Fireflies.

SECOND-LINE FLEET AIR ARM BARRACUDA SQUADRONS

Unit	Principal location(s)	Commission(s)
700 NAS	RNAS Worthy Down, Middle Wallop and Yeovilton	11/10/44–30/09/49 (Mk IIs 00/01/45–00/03/46, Mk IIIs 00/05/45–00/08/47)
703 NAS	RNAS Thorney Island, Lee-on-Solent and Ford	19/04/45–17/08/55 (Mk IIs 00/03/46–00/00/48, Mk IIIs 19/04/45–00/09/53)
706 NAS	RAAF Maryborough, Schofields and Nowra	06/03/45–31/05/46 (Mk IIs 00/08/45–00/03/46)
707 NAS	RNAS Burscough and Gosport	20/02/45–01/10/45 (Mk IIs and IIIs throughout)
710 NAS	RNAS Ronaldsway	07/10/44–20/12/45 (Mk IIs and IIIs throughout)
711 NAS	RNAS Crail	09/09/44–21/12/45 (Mk IIs throughout)
713 NAS	RNAS Ronaldsway	12/08/44–20/12/45 (Mk IIs throughout, Mk IIIs from 00/11/44)
714 NAS	RNAS Fearn and Rattray	01/08/44–29/10/45 (Mk IIs throughout, Mk IIIs from 00/10/44)
716 NAS	RNAS Eastleigh	28/06/44–01/09/45 (Mk IIs throughout)
717 NAS	RNAS Fearn and Rattray	01/07/44–22/03/46 (Mk IIs throughout)
719 NAS	RNAS Fearn and Eglinton and on board HMS *Implacable*	01/03/46–27/12/49 (Mk IIIs 01/03/46–00/05/49)
731 NAS	RNAS East Haven	05/12/43–01/11/45 (Mk IIs from 00/07/45)
733 NAS	RAF Minneriya and China Bay	01/01/44–31/12/47 (Mk IIs 01/09/44–00/07/45)
735 NAS	RNAS Burscough	01/08/43–30/04/46 (Mk IIs from 00/12/44, Mk IIIs from 00/11/45)
736 NAS	RNAS St Merryn	24/05/43–25/08/52 (Mk IIs 02/09/43–00/07/45)
737 NAS	RNAS Burscough	15/03/44–12/11/45 (Mk IIIs from 00/08/45)
744 NAS	RNAS Maydown and Eglinton	06/03/44–01/12/47 (Mk IIs 00/11/44–00/08/45, Mk IIIs 00/03/4–01/12/47)
747 NAS	RNAS Fearn, Inskip, Ronaldsway and Crail	22/03/43–20/12/45 (Mk Is 22/03/43–00/07/43, Mk IIs throughout, Mk IIIs 00/01/45–20/12/45)
750 NAS	RNAS Piarco (Trinidad); RNAS St Merryn in 1952	24/05/39–10/10/45, 17/04/52 to date (Mk IIs 00/11/44–10/10/45, Mk IIIs 17/04/52–00/07/53)

Left: By 1945, despite growing scepticism about the usefulness of the Barracuda for torpedo bombing (not least because of the paucity of targets in European and Atlantic waters at this stage of the war), training squadrons devoted to the art were still very active. Such was 710 NAS, one of whose Mk IIs is seen here taking off.

Right: The Fighter Combat School at Yeovilton and later St Merryn operated a large number of aircraft of differing capabilities, both in the offensive and the defensive rôles. Barracuda Mk IIs served for some two years in the latter (assigned to 736 Squadron), and LS633—here lacking radar, missing a fuselage panel and seen at St Merryn—was an example.

Commanding Officers	Remarks
Lt-Cdr L. R. E. Castlemaine RNVR, Cdr P. H. C. Illingworth (20/05/46)	Maintenance Test Pilot training unit.
Lt-Cdr J. H. Dundas DSC, Lt-Cdr J. C. N. Shrubsole DSC (25/04/47), Lt-Cdr W. R. J. MacWhirter DSC (22/04/48), Lt-Cdr N. A. Bartlett (08/05/50), Lt-Cdr J. M. Glaser DSC (25/04/51), Lt-Cdr S. M. de L. Longsden (08/01/53), Lt-Cdr F. J. Sherborne (20/07/53)	Naval Air–Sea Warfare Development Unit; later also Service Trials Unit (NASWDU/STU).
Lt-Cdr R. E. Bradshaw DSC**, Lt-Cdr D. M. R. Wynne-Roberts (31/08/45), Lt-Cdr C. A. Fraser (22/10/45)	Refresher training unit for aircrews serving with British Pacific Fleet.
Lt-Cdr S. S. Laurie RNVR	Naval School of Airborne Radar (formed out of 'B' Flight 735 NAS).
Lt-Cdr D. R. Connor RNVR, Lt-Cdr J. F. Arnold (01/08/45)	Torpedo training squadron.
Lt-Cdr J. B. Curgenven-Robinson DSC RNVR, Lt-Cdr D. M. Judd DSC RNVR (30/07/45)	Torpedo training squadron.
Lt-Cdr A. G. McWilliam RNVR	Torpedo bomber reconnaissance training squadron.
Lt-Cdr V. R. Crane RNVR, Lt P. D. Buckland RNVR (19/105/45)	Torpedo bomber reconnaissance training squadron.
Lt-Cdr J. F. Nicholas, Lt-Cdr D. V. Robinson RNVR (11/05/45)	School of Safety Equipment (specialising in air-sea rescue).
Lt-Cdr D. Norcock, Lt-Cdr A. Brunt DSC RNZVR (18/09/44), Lt-Cdr J. L. Fisher RNVR (26/01/45), Lt-Cdr H. T. T. Harding RNVR (21/12/45)	Torpedo bomber reconnaissance training squadron.
Lt-Cdr J. F. Arnold, Lt-Cdr C. R. J. Coxon (23/08/46), Lt-Cdr J. M. Brown (13/11/46), Lt-Cdr F. G. B. Sheffield DSC (08/01/47), Lt-Cdr R. H. W. Blake (08/12/47)	Strike (from 1947, anti-submarine) training squadron.
Lt-Cdr K. Stilliard RNVR, Lt-Cdr R. Pridham-Wippell (01/01/45)	Deck Landing Control Officer ('batsman') training unit.
Lt-Cdr L. Gilbert RNVR, Lt-Cdr J. A. Ansell RNVR (06/10/44)	Fleet requirements unit.
Lt-Cdr J. H. Mayne RNVR, Lt-Cdr S. L. Revett DSC RNVR (31/03/45), Lt-Cdr F. Stovin-Bradford DSC RNVR (31/03/45)	ASV radar training unit.
Lt-Cdr R. E. Gardner DSC RNVR, Lt-Cdr D. R. Curry DSC (17/08/44), Lt-Cdr P. D. Gick (08/02/45)	Fighter Combat School (part of School of Naval Air Warfare).
Lt-Cdr F. V. Jones RNVR	ASV radar training unit.
Lt-Cdr C. M. T. Hallewell RNVR, Lt-Cdr D. W. Phillips DSC (27/02/45), Lt J. H. B. Bedells (27/03/46), Lt R. H. W. Blake (20/05/46)	Merchant Aircraft Carrier ('MAC-ship') training unit; from summer 1945, anti-submarine training unit.
Lt-Cdr J. A. Ievers, Lt-Cdr F. A. Swanton DSC (13/09/43), Lt-Cdr T. M. Bassett RNZVR (01/03/44), Lt-Cdr R. D. Kingdon DSC RNVR (06/11/44)	Torpedo bomber reconnaissance pool and operational training unit.
Lt-Cdr J. H. Crook RNVR, Lt-Cdr H. Whitaker RNVR (15/03/45), Lt-Cdr F. B. Gardner RNVR (01/08/45); Lt-Cdr P. H. Fradd (17/04/52), Lt-Cdr E. F. Pritchard (19/01/53)	No 1 Observers' School.

continued . . .

BARRACUDA

Left, upper: A 736 Squadron Mk II airborne. This is DN633, one of only eighteen Barracudas built by Westland—although the original contract, before it was scaled back, called for 250.

Left, lower: As part of No 2 Observers' School, 753 Squadron flew Barracuda IIs towards the end of the war and for a short time thereafter. The 'A0' code—there is some debate about whether the '0' was a zero or a letter—signified RNAS Arbroath, where 753 was based for most of its existence; 'Q' was the individual aircraft identity letter.

Right: 750 Squadron had two 'bites' at the Barracuda, flying the Mk II towards the end of the war for observer training in Trinidad and re-forming with Mk IIIs in 1952, affiliated with 796 Squadron, for the same purpose. This is RJ797, at St Merryn in 1952.

Unit	Principal location(s)	Commission(s)
753 NAS	RNAS Rattray	24/05/39-09/08/46 (Mk IIs from 00/12/44)
756 NAS	RNAS Katukurunda	01/10/43-24/11/45 (Mk IIs 00/12/43-00/08/44), Mk IIIs 00/10/45-24/22/45
764 NAS	RNAS Gosport and Lee-on-Solent	19/02/44-01/09/45 (Mk IIs throughout)
767 NAS	RNAS East Haven	24/05/39-01/04/57 (Mk Is 00/06/44-00/08/44, Mk IIs 00/06/44-00/07/46)
768 NAS	RNAS Machrihanish, RAF Ayr and RNAS Abbotsinch and Ballyhalbert	13/01/41-16/04/46 (Mk Is 00/07/43-00/09/43), Mk IIs 00/07/43-00/10/45)
769 NAS	RNAS East Haven and Rattray	29/11/41-29/10/45 (Mk IIs from 00/11/43, Mk IIIs from 00/08/45)
774 NAS	RNAS St Merryn and Rattray	10/11/39-01/08/45 (Mk IIs from 00/02/44)
778 NAS	RNAS Arbroath, Crail, Gosport and Ford and RAF Tangmere	28/09/39-16/08/48 (Mk Is 00/05/42-00/11/43, Mk IIs 00/02/43-00/11/46, Mk IIIs 00/12/45-00/04/48, Mk Vs 00/09/46-00/07/47)

130

Commanding Officers	Remarks
Lt-Cdr R. E. Stewart RNVR, Lt-Cdr A. J. Phillips (12/08/45)	No 2 Observers' School (part).
Lt-Cdr A. D. Bourke RNVR, Lt W. E. Widdows (01/02/44), Lt-Cdr S. M. de L. Longsden (27/02/44), Lt-Cdr T. T. Miller (28/10/44), Lt-Cdr R. E. F. Kerrison RNVR (07/07/45), Lt-Cdr F. W. Baring RNVR (12/08/45)	Training and refresher unit.
Lt E. D. J. R. Whatley, Lt D. L. R. Hutchinson RNVR (19/04/44), Lt G. A. Donaghue RNVR (15/11/44), Capt. D. B. L. Smith RM (03/06 45)	User Trials Unit.
Lt-Cdr B. W. Vigrass RNVR, Lt-Cdr D. R. Park RNZVR (04/02/45), Lt-Cdr S. G. Cooke RNVR (12/08/45), Lt D. C. Hill MBE RNZVR (08/12/45), Lt-Cdr F. A. Swanton DSC* (22/01/46)	Deck landing training squadron.
Lt-Cdr J. S. Bailey, Lt-Cdr J. M. Brown DSC RNVR (19/10/44), Lt-Cdr R. Pridham-Wippell (01/11/45)	Deck landing training squadron.
Lt-Cdr P. N. Medd, Lt-Cdr D. Brooks DSC RNVR (08/07/44), Lt-Cdr G. C. Edwards RCNVR (07/04/45), Lt-Cdr G. Bennett DSC RNVR (28/06/45)	Deck landing training squadron.
Lt-Cdr P. P. Pardoe-Matthews RNR, Lt J. O. Sparke RNVR (07/10/44)	Armament training unit for observers and air gunners.
Lt-Cdr H. P. Bramwell DSO DSC, Lt-Cdr H. J. F. Lane (01/03/43), Lt-Cdr P. B. Schonfield (25/04/44), Lt-Cdr E. M. Britton (05/03/45), Lt-Cdr M. A. Lacayo (01/10/45), Lt-Cdr R. H. P. Carver DSC (03/07/46), Lt-Cdr F. R. A. Turnbull DSC* (16/01/48)	Service Trials Unit (from 1946 also Carrier Trials Unit).

continued . . .

Left: MD771 of 767 Squadron takes the wire on board HMS *Battler*, late summer or early autumn 1945. This unit was responsible for deck landing training—honing that vital skill demanded of all carrier-based pilots.

Right: A very near thing as LS535, a 769 Squadron Barracuda II, comes to a halt mere inches away from tipping over the side of the escort carrier HMS *Speaker*'s flight deck. The ship's safety barrier has been raised but has not been needed. Like 767 and 768 NAS, 769 was concerned with deck landing training.

BARRACUDA

Unit	Principal location(s)	Commission(s)
780 NAS	RNAS Lee-on-Solent	02/10/39–02/01/45 (Mk IIs 00/08/43–00/10/43)
781 NAS	RNAS Lee-on-Solent	20/03/40–31/07/45 (at least one Mk II on strength 00/05/43)
783 NAS	RNAS Arbroath and Lee-on-Solent	09/01/41–18/11/49 (Mk IIs 00/03/45–00/12/45, Mk IIIs 00/03/46–00/12/46, Mk Vs 00/12/47–00/10/48)
785 NAS	RNAS Crail	04/11/40–01/03/46 (Mk Is 00/12/42–00/01/44, Mk IIs 00/04/43–00/02/46, Mk IIIs in 00/02/46
786 NAS	RNAS Crail	21/11/40–21/12/45 (Mk Is 00/12/42–00/12/43, Mk IIs 00/12/43–00/12/45)
787 NAS	RAF Wittering and Tangmere	05/03/41–16/01/56 (Mk Is 00/04/43–00/06/43, Mk IIs 00/06/43–00/06/45)
796 NAS	RNAS St Merryn	13/11/47–01/10/58 (Mk IIIs 00/11/49–00/02/52)
797 NAS	RNAS Colombo Racecourse	00/07/42–24/10/45 (Mk IIs on strength 1944–45)
798 NAS	RNAS Lee-on-Solent and Stretton (detachment)	11/10/43–18/03/46 (Mk IIs 00/10/43–00/10/45, Mk IIIs 00/06/45–00/00/45)
799 NAS	RNAS Lee-on-Solent and on board HMS *Indefatigable*	30/07/45–12/08/52 (Mk IIIs 00/05/46–00/09/47)

Left: Barracuda II MX727 flying with the airborne lifeboat *in situ* (see also page 38). Such evaluation fell within the remit of 778 Squadron, as here, since this was a service trials unit. Notice the two smoke bombs nestling beneath the starboard wing, on the inboard rack. Below: 778 NAS was based at various shore stations during the war, but the carrier-compatibility trials it undertook were invariably conducted on board HMS *Pretoria Castle*, a British-built escort carrier and former passenger liner. Here one of the Squadron's Barracuda IIs leaves the deck.

Commanding Officers	Remarks
Lt-Cdr T. G. Stubley RNVR	Pilot conversion unit (esp. converting biplane pilots to monoplanes).
Lt-Cdr Sir George Lewis Bt RNVR	Communications unit.
Lt-Cdr T. B. Horsley RNVR, Lt W. L. M. Daubney RNVR (10/11/45), Lt E. H. G. Child RNVR (10/12/45), Lt-Cdr A. M. Tuke (01/12/46), Lt-Cdr K. C. Winstanley (01/12/47), Lt-Cdr G. H. Colles (27/05/48)	ASV radar training squadron.
Lt-Cdr K. G. Sharp, Lt-Cdr M. Thorpe (01/07/43), Lt-Cdr R. B. Lunberg (31/01/44), Lt-Cdr M. W. Rudorf DSC (05/12/44), Lt-Cdr L. C. Watson DSC (13/06/45), Lt-Cdr N. V. Haigh RNVR (31/07/45), Lt-Cdr J. F. Arnold (15/12/45)	Torpedo bomber reconnaissance training squadron.
Lt-Cdr B. E. Boulding DSC, Lt-Cdr D. Norcock (10/08/43), Lt-Cdr R. J. Fisher RNZVR (30/06/44), Lt-Cdr F. H. Franklin RNZVR (30/10/44), Lt-Cdr L. C. Watson DSC (13/06/45)	Torpedo bomber reconnaissance training squadron.
Cdr B. H. M. Kendall OBE	Naval Air Fighting Development Unit.
Lt-Cdr R. D. Henderson, Lt-Cdr T. J. Harris (18/12/50), Lt-Cdr S. E. Adams (07/12/51), Lt-Cdr J. S. Barnes (16/01/52)	Aircrewmen training; from 1950, Observers' School Part II.
Lt-Cdr K. C. Winstanley RNVR	Fleet requirements unit.
Lt-Cdr I. J. Wallace OBE RNVR, Lt-Cdr S. W. Birse DSC RNR (08/08/45)	Advanced aircrew conversion unit.
Lt-Cdr N. R. Quill RNR, Lt-Cdr P. W. Compton DSC (04/11/46), Lt-Cdr J. B. Harrowar DFC RNVR (01/07/47)	Refresher and conversion squadron.

Right and below: 778 and 783 Naval Air Squadrons were the only units ever to be equipped with the Barracuda Mk V, although a couple of the aircraft were also used as general workhorses in Ships' Flights. Some Mk IIIs were also used in this way (see later), the relatively capacious interiors of the aircraft being advantageous. A Mk V from 783 NAS, RK558, is shown, the extended, squared-off wing tips of the variant being particularly apparent in the photograph below.

BARRACUDA

ROYAL AIR FORCE BARRACUDA SQUADRONS

Unit	Principal location(s)	Equipment	Remarks
No 567 Squadron	RAF Detling, Hornchurch and Hawkinge	Mk IIs 00/12/43–00/07/45	Anti-aircraft co-operation.
No 618 Squadron	RAF Skitten	Mk IIs 00/07/44–00/12/44	Deck landing training in association with Mosquito 'Highball' sorties.
No 667 Squadron	RNAS Gosport	Mk IIs 00/05/44–00/06/45	Target-towing and anti-aircraft co-operation.
No 679 Squadron	RAF Ipswich	Mk IIs 00/03/44–00/06/45	Anti-aircraft co-operation.
No 691 Squadron	RAF Roborough and Harrowbeer	Mk IIs 00/01/44–00/03/45	Anti-aircraft co-operation.

MISCELLANEOUS BARRACUDA UNITS

Aeroplane & Armament Experimental Establishment	Boscombe Down	Mk Is, IIs, IIIs and Vs 00/10/41–00/00/47	Trials and evaluation.
Royal Aircraft Establishment	Farnborough	Mk Is, IIs, IIIs and Vs 00/00/41–00/00/46	Trials and evaluation.
Air Torpedo Development Unit	RNAS Gosport	Mk IIIs 00/05/49–00/12/52	Torpedo-dropping trials.
RN Air Station Flights	RNAS East Haven and Gosport	Mk IIs 00/00/45–00/00/47	General communications duties.
RN Ships' Flights	HM Ships *Illustrious*, *Formidable*, *Indomitable*, *Implacable*, *Indefatigable*, *Vengeance* and *Premier*	Various marks at various times 00/00/44–00/00/51	General communications duties.
Escadron de Liaison Aérienne 56 (*Aéronavale*)	Persan-Beaumont, Algiers	Mk IIs (ASH) 00/03/48–00/00/56)	Covert operations.

Below: Another view of Barracuda P9795/G (see page 39), which was evaluated by the A&AEE at Boscombe Down after the war. Two paratroopers could be accommodated—rather uncomfortably, one imagines—in each nacelle, with equipment carried in an underbelly pod, but the project was assessed to be of little practical value and abandoned.
Opposite, top: RJ925, in silver finish, of the Air Torpedo Development Unit, having made a forced landing at RNAS Culdrose on 29 May 1951. The aircraft is a Mk 3, although the latter's characteristic ventral radome is missing—presumably surplus to requirements (and probably a physical encroachment) during torpedo-dropping trials. Following this incident, RJ925 was repaired and returned to service.
Opposite, centre: Barracuda Mk II MX613 fitted for airborne lifeboat trials at A&AEE Boscombe Down in 1945.
Opposite, bottom: The Barracuda Mk 3 of HMS *Indomitable*'s Ship's Flight ('A' is carried on the fin) in June 1952; notice the two Sea Hornet N.F.21s of 809 Squadron in the background. The aircraft is probably RJ911, and, again, the radome has been removed, while the paintwork along the wing leading edge shows a fair degree of erosion.

COURTESY PHILIP JARRETT

BARRACUDA SQUADRONS

Above: RK409, a Barracuda II presented on board HMS *Theseus* during October 1946 when the carrier docked in Liverpool for an 'At Home' week. The aircraft, posed on the ship's accelerator and sporting an inert torpedo, was part of a display of representative FAA aircraft, and although RK409 has been referred to as belonging to *Theseus*'s Ship's Flight, there is no evidence that it actually served in this capacity. It is not clear whether the inscription 'Queen Elizabeth' refers to Her Majesty (the consort of King George VI) or the Cunard passenger liner. *Flight* magazine reported on the event, noting somewhat indignantly that the 'elderly Seafires [on board at the time] were recklessly exposed to the wrenching grasp and hammering tread of Liverpool youth.'

Left, top: Barracuda Mk V RK571 while serving with the Ship's Flight on board HMS *Implacable* in 1948. The location here is RNAS Culdrose.

Left, centre: Mk V RK568 also served with *Implacable*'s Ship's Flight, and was RK571's predecessor. It was dubbed 'Pony Express' (the name is just visible beneath the massive Griffon exhaust outlet).

Left, bottom: Mk II BV733 was dispatched to NAS Patuxent River for evaluation by the US Navy and is seen here at that base in December 1943.

136

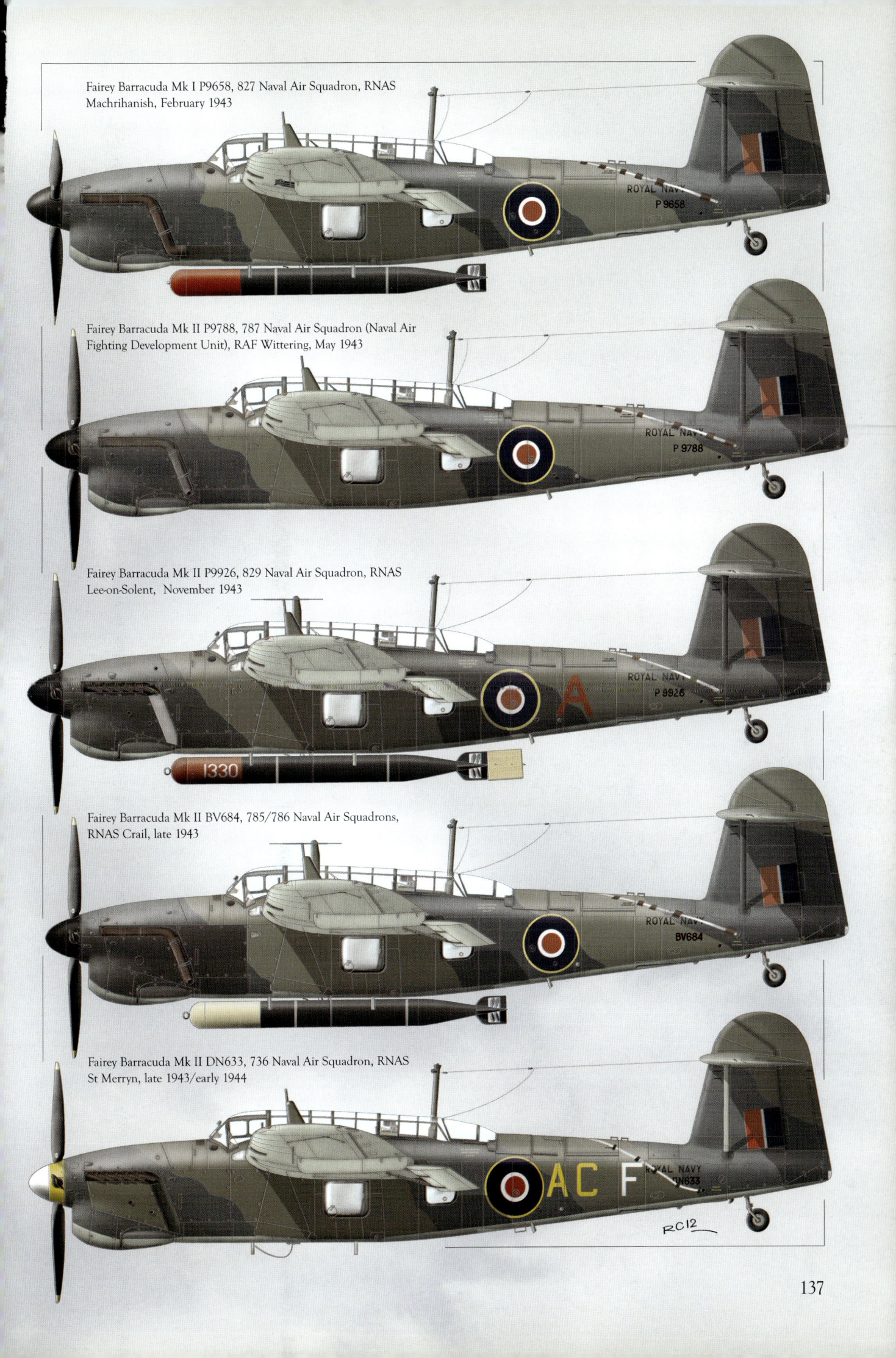

Fairey Barracuda Mk I P9658, 827 Naval Air Squadron, RNAS
Machrihanish, February 1943

Fairey Barracuda Mk II P9788, 787 Naval Air Squadron (Naval Air
Fighting Development Unit), RAF Wittering, May 1943

Fairey Barracuda Mk II P9926, 829 Naval Air Squadron, RNAS
Lee-on-Solent, November 1943

Fairey Barracuda Mk II BV684, 785/786 Naval Air Squadrons,
RNAS Crail, late 1943

Fairey Barracuda Mk II DN633, 736 Naval Air Squadron, RNAS
St Merryn, late 1943/early 1944

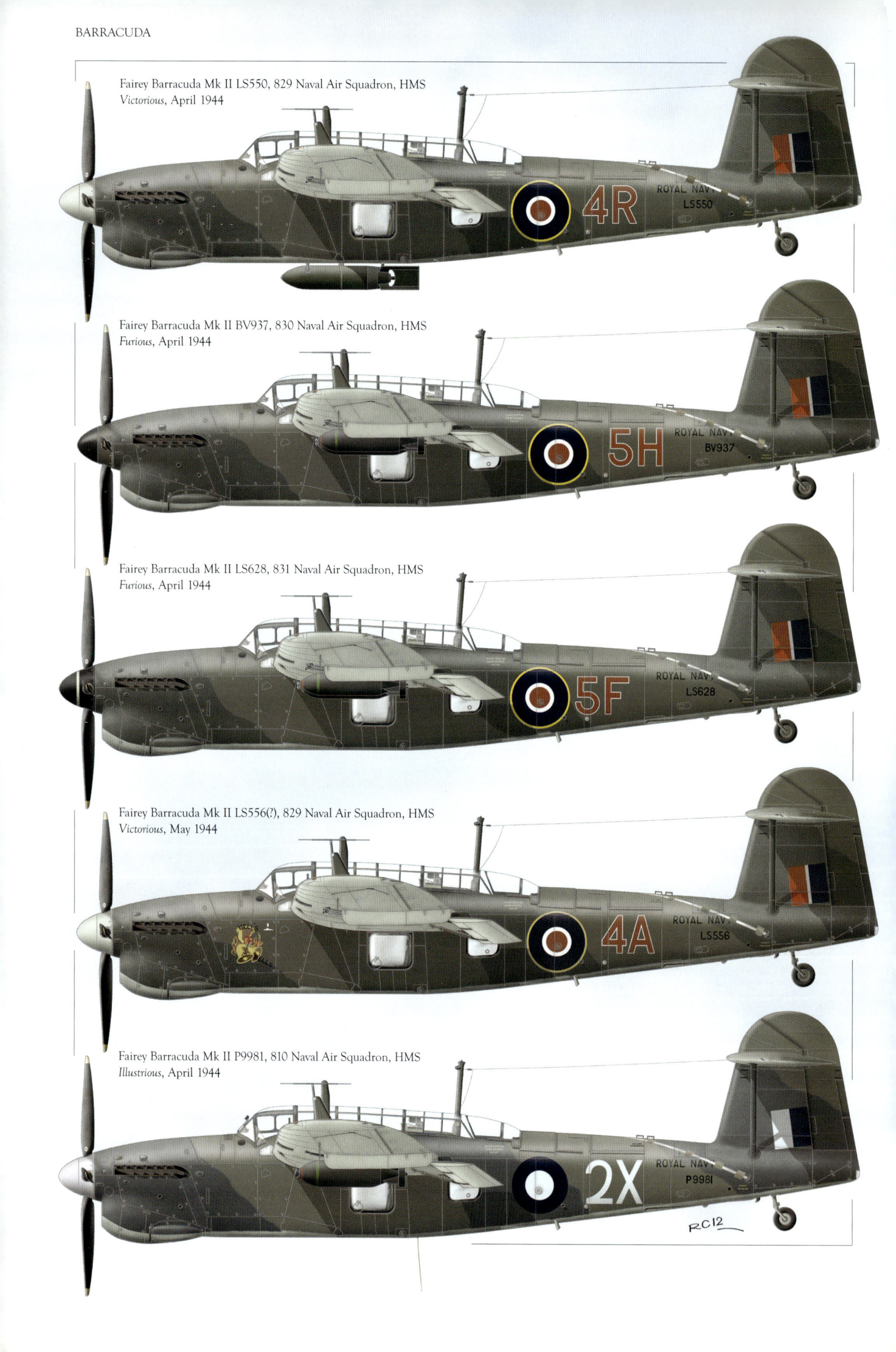

BARRACUDA

Fairey Barracuda Mk II LS550, 829 Naval Air Squadron, HMS *Victorious*, April 1944

Fairey Barracuda Mk II BV937, 830 Naval Air Squadron, HMS *Furious*, April 1944

Fairey Barracuda Mk II LS628, 831 Naval Air Squadron, HMS *Furious*, April 1944

Fairey Barracuda Mk II LS556(?), 829 Naval Air Squadron, HMS *Victorious*, May 1944

Fairey Barracuda Mk II P9981, 810 Naval Air Squadron, HMS *Illustrious*, April 1944

Fairey Barracuda Mk II LS503, 817 Naval Air Squadron, HMS *Indomitable*, August 1944

Fairey Barracuda Mk II, serial number unconfirmed, 711 Naval Air Squadron, RNAS Crail, late 1944

Fairey Barracuda Mk II (ASH) MX724, 817 Naval Air Squadron, RNAS Fearn, May 1945

Fairey Barracuda Mk III PM933, 810 Naval Air Squadron, RAF Beccles, May 1945

Fairey Barracuda Mk II PM834, 814 Naval Air Squadron, RNAS Katukurunda, June 1945

BARRACUDA

140

SQUADRONS AND COLOURS

FLOWN BY THE AUTHOR

FAIREY BARRACUDA Mk II
PM821, 827 Naval Air Squadron, HMS *Colossus*, January 1946

Note: The configuration shown here is not typical of wartime Barracudas: there are a number of 'local' modifications, including the removal of the ASV radar and the replacement of the observer's blister windows with sheet Perspex. The port wing tip and main port engine panels are replacements, not matching the overall camouflage paint finish, while the Sky nose panels and wing leading edges are also non-standard. The TAG's guns are also absent (as indeed was the TAG himself).

141

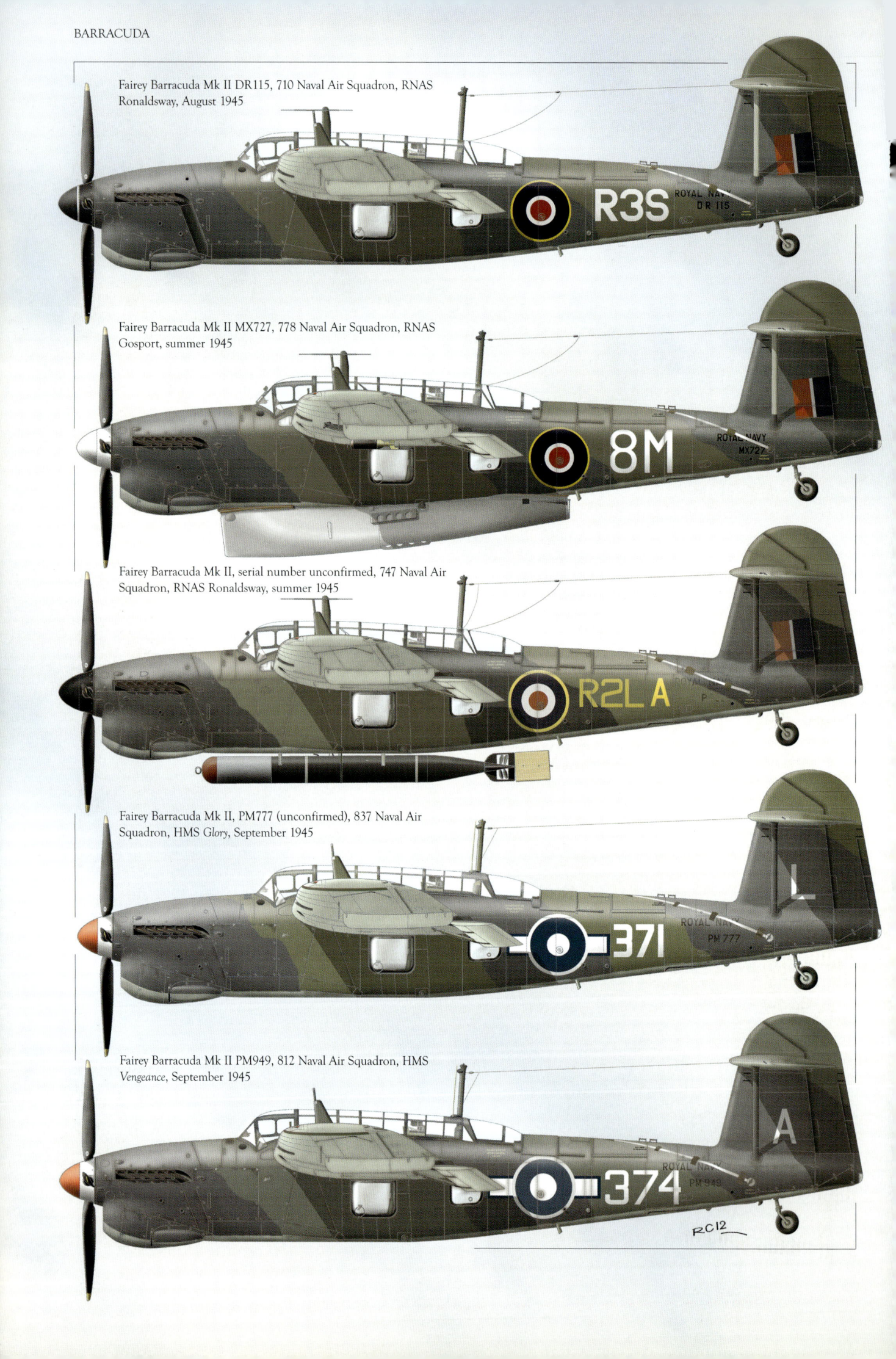

BARRACUDA

Fairey Barracuda Mk II DR115, 710 Naval Air Squadron, RNAS Ronaldsway, August 1945

Fairey Barracuda Mk II MX727, 778 Naval Air Squadron, RNAS Gosport, summer 1945

Fairey Barracuda Mk II, serial number unconfirmed, 747 Naval Air Squadron, RNAS Ronaldsway, summer 1945

Fairey Barracuda Mk II, PM777 (unconfirmed), 837 Naval Air Squadron, HMS *Glory*, September 1945

Fairey Barracuda Mk II PM949, 812 Naval Air Squadron, HMS *Vengeance*, September 1945

Fairey Barracuda Mk III RJ909, 744 Naval Air Squadron, RNAS Eglinton, October 1945

Fairey Barracuda Mk II RK479, Ship's Flight HMS *Vengeance*, June 1947

Fairey Barracuda Mk V RK558, 783 Naval Air Squadron, RNAS Lee-on-Solent, March 1948

Fairey Barracuda Mk V RK568, Ship's Flight HMS *Implacable*, April 1948

Fairey Barracuda Mk V RK571, Ship's Flight HMS *Implacable*, June 1948

BARRACUDA

Fairey Barracuda Mk 3 RJ765, Ship's Flight HMS *Indomitable*, March 1951

Fairey Barracuda Mk 3 RJ925, Aircraft Torpedo Development Unit, RNAS Gosport, May 1951

Fairey Barracuda Mk 3 RJ933, 815 Naval Air Squadron, RNAS Eglinton, November 1951

Fairey Barracuda Mk 3 ME183, 796 Naval Air Squadron, RNAS St Merryn, March 1952

Fairey Barracuda Mk 3 RJ797, 750 Naval Air Squadron, RNAS St Merryn, August 1952